The Microwave Convection Oven Cookbook

Contents

PRECAUTIONS TO AVOID POSSIBLE EXPOSURE TO EXCESSIVE MICROWAVE ENERGY

(a) **Do not attempt to operate this oven with the door open** since open-door operation can result in harmful exposure to microwave energy. It is important not to defeat or tamper with the safety interlocks.

(b) **Do not place any object** between the oven front face and the door or allow soil or cleaner residue to accumulate on sealing surfaces.

(c) **Do not operate the oven** if it is damaged. It is particularly important that the oven door close properly and that there is no damage to the:
   (1) door (bent)
   (2) hinges and latches (broken or loosened)
   (3) door seals and sealing surfaces

(d) **The oven should not be adjusted or repaired** by anyone except properly qualified service personnel.

◄ *Chicken A La Roma;*
for recipe, see p. 51

Introduction

Microwave

In microwave ovens, household electricity is converted into a type of high frequency radiowave by a magnetron tube. These microwaves cause the water molecules within the food to vibrate at extremely high speeds. This friction produces the intense heat which cooks the food.

Unlike in conventional ovens, foods cooked in the microwave oven are placed directly on the oven floor.

One advantage of microwave cooking is that food can be heated directly in the serving utensil. Not all serving utensils are microwave oven safe. Check manufacturer's recommendation before using.

Convection

As in a conventional oven, the convection oven has a heating element necessary to produce crisp, brown exteriors. However, in a convection oven a fan is used to circulate the hot air which results in more uniform cooking.

The metal accessory rack is placed directly on oven floor during all convection cooking.

When baking cookies in this oven, the best results are obtained by using the convection setting. The circulation of hot air during convection cooking gives cookies crisp, brown exteriors along with chewy interiors.

Combination

During combination cooking, the oven automatically alternates between convection and microwave heating. Combination cooking gives the advantage of convection browning and the speed of microwaving.

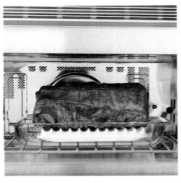

Combination cooking is ideal for roasting meat. The circulating hot air quickly browns the meat sealing in the juices which reduces shrinkage.

When cooking by combination, casseroles require less time than when conventionally cooked and less attention than when microwaved.

Utensil

The type of utensil used will depend upon the cooking method selected. Although there is cookware on the market specifically designed for use in combination ovens, there is no need to purchase new utensils. Always check the manufacturer's recommendation before use.

Paper, glass and microwave-safe plastic utensils are ideal for use in microwave ovens.

To make sure a dish is microwave safe, place it in the oven. Put 1 cup water in a glass measure. Place beside dish and microwave 1 minute. If dish remains cool, it is suitable for microwaving.

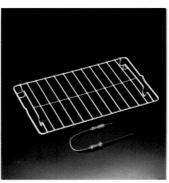

This oven comes equipped with several accessories including a metal accessory rack and probe. Consult charts and recipes for recommended use of each accessory.

Utensils which are normally used in a conventional oven can also be used when convection cooking.

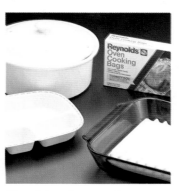

Combination cookware must be heat resistant up to 400°F. Oven-safe glassware and ceramic dishes are ideal for combination cooking.

Cookware and Utensil Guide

TIPS: 1. Always check the manufacturer's recommendation before using any utensils in the oven.
2. Check utensil size to make sure it will fit in the oven.

Type of Utensil	Microwave	Convection	Combination	Broil†
Aluminum Foil	For Shielding	Yes	For Shielding	Yes
Browning Dish	Yes	No	No	No
Brown Paper Bags	No	No	No	No
Dinnerware				
Oven/Microwave Safe	Yes	Yes	Yes	No
Non Oven/Microwave Safe	Yes	No	No	No
Disposable Polyester				
Paperboard Dishes	Yes	Yes* heat resistant up to 400°F	Yes* heat resistant up to 400°F	No
Glassware				
Oven Glassware & Ceramic	Yes	Yes	Yes	No
Non Heat Resistant	No	No	No	No
Metal Accessory Rack	No	Yes	Yes	Yes
Metal Cookware	No	Yes	No	Yes
Metal Twist-Ties	No	Yes	No	No
Oven Cooking Bag	Yes	Yes	Yes	No
Paper Towels and Napkins	Yes**	No	No	No
Plastic Dishes				
Microwave Safe	Yes	Yes* heat resistant up to 400°F	Yes* heat resistant up to 400°F	No
Plastic Wrap	Yes	No	No	No
Straw, Wicker, Wood	Yes	No	No	No
Thermometers				
Microwave Safe	Yes	No	No	No
Conventional	No	Yes	No	Yes
Wax Paper	Yes	No	No	No

* Always check manufacturer's recommendation.

** Do not use paper towels which contain synthetic fiber woven into them such as nylon. Synthetic fibers may cause the towel to ignite.

† For ovens so equipped.

Microwave Techniques

The characteristics of food and the application of certain techniques will influence the speed and effectiveness of microwave cooking. While the techniques may be familiar, the way they are used may be somewhat different because of the unique way in which microwave energy cooks.

STARTING TEMPERATURE Suggested cook times in this book are based on normal storage temperatures. Foods which are refrigerated or frozen may require longer cooking time than foods stored at room temperature.

DENSITY In both conventional and microwave cooking, dense foods, such as potatoes, take longer to cook or reheat than light porous foods such as a piece of cake, bread or a roll.

MOISTURE CONTENT Moisture of food affects how it cooks. Very moist foods cook evenly because microwave energy is attracted to water molecules. Food with low moisture content should be covered during cooking and allowed to stand after cooking so heat can disperse evenly.

QUANTITY In microwave cooking, where time is directly related to the number of servings, small amounts of food take less time to cook than large ones.

SIZE Foods which are similar in size and shape cook more evenly. Small pieces cook faster than large ones. When cooking large pieces of food such as a roast, the power level may be reduced to allow for more even cooking.

STIRRING When microwaving, for best results, stir foods from the outside to the center of the dish once or twice during cooking. Foods which require constant stirring conventionally will need only occasional stirring. When possible, stir foods before serving.

ROTATING Repositioning a dish in the oven may help foods cook evenly. To rotate ½ turn, turn the dish until the side which was to the back of the oven is to the front. To rotate ¼ turn, turn the dish until the side which was to the back of the oven is to the side.

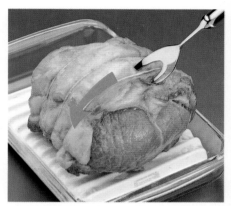

TURNING OVER When microwaving, turning over or rearranging is often needed to allow for even heating of foods. Turning large cuts of meat or frozen hamburgers over once or twice during cooking will give best results.

STAND TIME In microwaving, stand time is necessary to allow foods to finish cooking. During stand time, moist surface areas on cakes will disappear and the internal temperature of a roast will continue to rise. Most recipes require stand times ranging from 5 to 15 minutes.

TEMPERATURE Foods with delicate textures are best cooked at lower power levels. Using the temperature probe can prevent milk-based liquids from over cooking. To ensure thorough heating, foods should reach a temperature of 160°F to 165°F before serving.

DO NOT MICROWAVE. Do not cook eggs in shells. Avoid heating foods in narrow necked jars and bottles. Always remove lids from wide necked jars before warming food. Heating baby food in jars is not recommended.

Microwave Techniques

Microwaves pass through paper, glass, plastic and ceramic utensils. These materials are ideal for microwave oven cooking because they allow microwave energy to penetrate the food. Paper towels and napkins absorb moisture in foods like bacon and aid in retaining moisture in foods such as breads and rolls.

Microwaves are reflected by metal. Foil wrapped boxes, aluminum containers deeper than ¾ inch, metal baking utensils and conventional meat thermometers are not suitable for use in microwave ovens. Do not use glass, pottery or pyroceram utensils with metal trim or fittings.

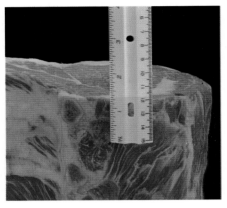

Microwaves penetrate to a depth of about ¾ to 1¼ inches. This microwave energy causes molecules within the food to vibrate, producing the heat necessary to cook the food.

Foods should be arranged with the meatiest portions around the outer edge of the dish and thinner pieces towards the middle. This enables thick portions to cook completely without overcooking thin pieces.

Size and shape of a container will influence the microwave cooking time. A shallow casserole exposes more food surface to microwave energy and will require less time to cook than taller utensils holding the same amount. Since microwaves penetrate from all sides, round shapes and rings cook more evenly.

Today many convenience foods are packaged in containers designed especially for use in microwave ovens. Consult package instructions for cooking procedures.

PRICK FOODS TO RELEASE PRESSURE. Steam causes pressure to build in foods which are tightly covered by a skin or membrane. Prick potatoes, egg yolks and chicken livers to prevent bursting.

ARRANGEMENT Place individual items, like custard cups or baked potatoes in a ring. Allow space between foods so energy can penetrate from all sides.

SHIELDING When microwave cooking or defrosting, foods may be shielded to prevent overcooking. Use small strips of foil to shield thin parts, such as the tips of wings and legs on poultry, which may cook before larger parts.

SHAPE OF FOOD When microwaving, arrange foods with the thickest or less tender portions to the outside of the dish. This prevents thinner more tender pieces from overcooking. Arrange foods of equal size in a ring, leaving the center empty.

COVERING To cook quickly and retain moisture, cover dish with a lid or plastic wrap. Vent plastic wrap by turning back one edge to form a narrow slot where excess steam can escape. To hold in heat and prevent spatters without steaming, use wax paper.

POROUS COVERS Paper towels or napkins allow steam to escape, absorb moisture and prevent spattering.

Defrosting Techniques

See Pages 130-131 For Defrosting Chart.

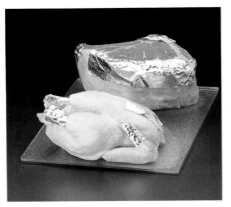

Casseroles, soups and stews will require stirring once or twice during defrosting. Layered casseroles that cannot be stirred, such as lasagna, should be rotated several times to allow for more even defrosting.

Remove meat from the original wrapper and place in baking dish. Defrost for first half of time. Break up or separate ground beef, steaks, chops, chicken pieces or fish fillets after half of defrosting time. Remove any defrosted pieces and return remainder to oven to continue defrosting. If additional thawing is needed, return frozen portions to oven to complete defrosting.

Turn large roasts, whole chickens and cornish hens over after half of defrosting time. Shield warm areas with small pieces of foil. For whole poultry, start with the breast side down; shield legs and wing tips after turning over. Defrost meats and poultry only until they can be pierced to the center with a skewer. The surface should feel cool but not icy.

Power Level Chart

Power Level		Percent of Power
HIGH	(10)	100%
	(9)	90%
	(8)	80%
MEDIUM HIGH	(7)	70%
	(6)	60%
MEDIUM	(5)	50%
	(4)	40%
LOW/DEFROST	(3)	30%
	(2)	20%
WARM	(1)	10%

Delicate foods such as cheesecake, frosted cakes or cream pies should be removed from original wrapper and placed on a serving plate. Microwave at LOW (3), until a wooden pick can be inserted in the center easily. Let cakes and pies stand 15 to 25 minutes before serving.

Microwave Adapting

When adapting recipes for the microwave, it is best to start with a familiar recipe. Knowing how the food should look and taste will help when adapting it for microwaving. Foods that require browning or crisp, dry surfaces will cook best when using the convection or combination setting.

- Refer to similar microwave recipes for cooking techniques, power levels and microwaving time.

- Moist foods such as vegetables, fruits, poultry and seafood microwave well.

- Rich foods such as bar cookies, moist cakes and candies are suitable for microwaving because of their high fat and sugar content.

- Reduce conventional cooking time by one-third to one-half. Check food after minimum time to avoid overcooking.

- Small amounts of butter or oil can be used for flavoring but are not needed to prevent sticking.

- Seasonings may need to be reduced. Salt meats and vegetables after cooking.

- Liquids may need to be reduced.

Recipe Conversion

Conventional Spanish Rice

1 lb. ground beef
1 ½ cups water
¾ cup long grain rice
2 tablespoons chili powder
2 tablespoons instant minced onion
1 teaspoon salt
⅛ teaspoon pepper
1 (28 oz.) can whole tomatoes, cut up

In 10-in. skillet, crumble ground beef. Cook over medium high heat 10 minutes, uncovered. Add water, rice, chili powder, onion, salt, pepper and tomatoes. Mix well. Cover and cook over medium heat 35 to 40 minutes.

Total Cooking Time 45 to 50 Minutes
Serves 4 to 6

Microwave Spanish Rice

1 lb. ground chuck
1 cup uncooked instant rice
2 tablespoons chili powder
1 tablespoon instant minced onion
1 teaspoon salt
⅛ teaspoon pepper
1 (28 oz.) can whole tomatoes, cut up

In 2-qt. casserole, crumble beef. Add instant rice, chili powder, minced onions, salt, pepper and tomatoes. Mix well. Cover. Microwave at HIGH (10) 12 to 14 minutes, stirring after 6 minutes. If top of food appears dry during cooking, stir again. Return to oven to finish cooking.

Total Cooking Time 12 to 14 Minutes
Serves 4 to 6

CONVENTIONAL

MICROWAVE

Introduction

Convection Cooking

In a convection oven, a fan circulates hot air around the food and evenly distributes it throughout the oven cavity. The circulating air uniformly heats the food producing a crisp, brown exterior. In most cases, convection baking and roasting temperatures will be the same as those recommended for conventional cooking. Refer to individual charts and recipes for best baking temperatures.

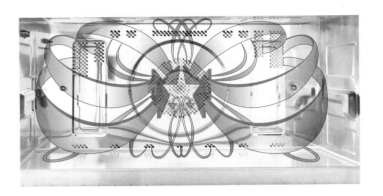

Convection Techniques

Many of the techniques used in conventional cooking are also important when cooking by convection. Following these recommendations will assure exceptional baking results.

The same cookware and utensils that are normally used when conventionally baking can also be used in convection ovens. For best results, however, use shiny, aluminum utensils.

Dark or matte finish utensils will produce darker browning on food surfaces.

Heat-resistant paper and plastic containers that manufacturers recommend for use in conventional ovens can be used in convection ovens. Plastic cooking utensils that are heat resistant to temperatures of 400°F are also suitable.

Use a pan with low sides whenever possible. A shallow pan allows air to circulate around the food more efficiently.

As a general rule, convection baking temperatures will be the same as those used in a conventional oven.

Remember, oven walls, shelves and cooking utensils do get hot during convection cooking. Always use dry oven mitts when removing utensils from the oven.

Combination

Combination cooking combines the best features of convection and microwave. Foods cook quickly with less manipulation than when microwaved and achieve the crisp, brown exterior of convection cooking. When combination cooking, reduce conventional cooking times by one-fourth to one-third. Always check for doneness at minimum time.

Glass baking dishes, stoneware and pottery utensils designed for use in both conventional and microwave ovens, may be used for combination cooking.

Convenience foods packaged in heat-resistant paper and plastic containers that are recommended for use in conventional ovens can also be used when combination cooking. Plastic cooking utensils that are heat resistant to a temperature of 400°F are also suitable.

When checking foods for doneness in the combination oven use conventional techniques. For example, cake is done when a toothpick inserted in the center comes out clean. The top will also appear dry and spring back when touched lightly.

Aluminum cake pans and utensils are not recommended for use in combination cooking. Paper products and plastic utensils, recommended for microwave use only, cannot be used in combination cooking. Always check the manufacturer's recommendations.

Convection Results

Any food that can be cooked in a conventional oven, cooks beautifully in a convection oven. In fact, professional chefs choose convection ovens for consistently superior baking and roasting results.

Convection roasting is ideal for meats. Moisture and flavor are sealed in quickly as circulating hot air browns the surface.

Chicken and other poultry develop crisp golden skin but stay juicy and tender.

Casseroles may bake in less time or at a lower temperature than in a conventional oven.

Pies baked in a convection oven are evenly browned, tender and flaky.

The convection oven's uniform temperature helps keep airy foods, such as cream puffs, high and light.

Breads baked in the convection oven have consistent texture and evenly browned crusts.

Appetizers & Beverages

Garlic Shrimp

2 tablespoons butter
2 cloves garlic, minced
¼ lb. fresh medium shrimp, peeled and deveined
1½ teaspoons fresh parsley, snipped
1½ teaspoons grated Parmesan cheese

In small mixing bowl, combine butter and garlic. Microwave at HIGH (10) 1 to 2 minutes. Add shrimp and parsley. Microwave at MEDIUM HIGH (7) 1 to 2 minutes; stir after 30 seconds. Stir in Parmesan cheese.

Total Microwave Cooking Time 2 to 4 Minutes
Makes 4 appetizer servings

Oriental Meatballs

1 lb. ground beef
1 lb. ground pork
½ cup canned water chestnuts, drained, finely chopped
¼ cup green pepper, finely chopped
3 green onions, chopped
2 tablespoons soy sauce
2 tablespoons pineapple juice
Sauce:
1 (20 oz.) can chunk pineapple, undrained
1 tablespoon instant beef bouillon granules
¼ cup brown sugar, packed
2 tablespoons cornstarch
1 tablespoon soy sauce
2 tablespoons vinegar
⅔ cup water

In large mixing bowl, combine beef, pork, water chestnuts, green pepper, onions, soy sauce and pineapple juice; mix well. Shape into 1-inch meatballs. Arrange in 2-quart oblong glass baking dish. Cover with wax paper. Microwave at HIGH (10) 7 to 9 minutes until meats are thoroughly cooked; rearrange after 6 minutes. Drain meatballs and set aside.

Drain pineapple, reserving liquid. In 4-cup glass measure, combine reserved pineapple juice, beef bouillon, brown sugar, cornstarch, soy sauce, vinegar and water. Microwave at HIGH (10) 4 to 5 minutes, until mixture thickens; stir after 2 minutes. Add pineapple. Pour sauce over meatballs. Microwave at HIGH (10) 3 to 4 minutes until heated through.

Total Microwave Cooking Time 14 to 18 Minutes
Makes 45 to 50 meatballs

Cheese Ball

¼ cup butter
1 (3 oz.) pkg. cream cheese
1 teaspoon Worcestershire sauce
½ teaspoon onion powder
⅛ teaspoon garlic powder
3 cups Cheddar cheese, shredded
½ cup walnuts, finely chopped or fresh parsley, snipped
Assorted crackers

Place butter in 1-cup glass measure. Microwave at HIGH (10) 15 to 20 seconds until butter softens. Place cream cheese in 2-quart glass mixing bowl. Microwave at MEDIUM (5) 30 to 40 seconds until cream cheese softens. Blend in softened butter, Worcestershire sauce, onion powder, garlic powder and Cheddar cheese. Beat at medium speed of electric mixer until smooth. Shape into ball. Roll in nuts or parsley to coat. Refrigerate for 3 hours. Serve with crackers.

Total Microwave Cooking Time ¾ to 1 Minute
Makes one 4-inch cheese ball

◄ *Garlic Shrimp*

Appetizers & Beverages

▲ *Vegetable Crispers, Spicy Chicken Wings and Cocktail Reubens*

Place buttered vegetables into plastic bag with crumb mixture and shake to coat evenly.

Vegetable Crispers

½ **cup dry bread crumbs**
½ **cup grated Parmesan cheese**
1 **teaspoon tarragon leaves, crushed**
1 **teaspoon paprika**
Dash pepper
1 **cup broccoli flowerets**
1 **cup cauliflower flowerets**
1 **medium zucchini, sliced ½-inch thick**
12 **small whole mushrooms**
½ **cup butter, melted**

Combine bread crumbs, Parmesan cheese, tarragon, paprika and pepper in plastic bag. Taking several pieces at a time, dip broccoli, cauliflower, zucchini and mushrooms in melted butter. Place into plastic bag with crumb mixture and shake to coat evenly. Repeat until all vegetables are coated. Arrange in single layer in lightly greased 3-quart oblong glass baking dish. Place metal accessory rack on floor of oven. Preheat oven to 350°F. Convection Bake 15 to 18 minutes or until lightly browned.

Total Convection Cooking Time 15 to 18 Minutes
Makes about 40 appetizers

Cocktail Reubens

36 slices cocktail rye bread,
   toasted
½ cup Thousand Island
   dressing
1 (8 oz.) can sauerkraut,
   rinsed and drained
¼ lb. thinly-sliced corned
   beef
1 (6 oz.) pkg. Swiss cheese
   slices, each slice cut into
   4 squares

Arrange bread slices on baking sheet. Spread each slice with about ¾ teaspoon Thousand Island dressing. Add small amount of sauerkraut and corned beef to each slice. Top each with 1 square Swiss cheese. Place metal accessory rack on floor of oven. Preheat oven to 350°F. Convection Bake 5 to 8 minutes or until cheese melts and edges are lightly browned.

Total Convection Cooking Time 5 to 8 Minutes
Makes 36 appetizers

Spicy Chicken Wings

½ cup sour cream
2 tablespoons red onion,
   finely chopped
1 clove garlic, crushed
¼ cup fresh parsley,
   minced
1 cup mayonnaise
¼ cup blue cheese,
   crumbled
1 tablespoon lemon juice
¼ teaspoon seasoned salt
¼ teaspoon freshly ground
   black pepper
⅛ teaspoon cayenne pepper
½ cup butter, melted
1 teaspoon hot sauce
25 chicken wings, separated
   into 2 pieces

In small mixing bowl, combine sour cream, onion, garlic, parsley, mayonnaise, blue cheese, lemon juice, seasoned salt, pepper and cayenne pepper. Mix well and refrigerate.

Place metal accessory rack on floor of oven. Preheat oven to 350°F. In small mixing bowl, combine melted butter and hot sauce. Place chicken wings in 3-quart oblong glass baking dish. Brush wings with butter mixture. Convection Bake 25 to 30 minutes until golden brown. Serve with refrigerated dip.

Total Convection Cooking Time 25 to 30 Minutes
Makes 5 to 6 appetizer servings

Appetizers & Beverages

▲ *Sausage Muffin Teasers and Tiny Chicken Turnovers*

Sausage Muffin Teasers

½ lb. hot bulk pork
   sausage
2 cups all-purpose flour
1 tablespoon baking
   powder
1 tablespoon sugar
¼ teaspoon salt
⅛ teaspoon thyme
Dash cayenne pepper
1 cup milk
1 egg, slightly beaten
¼ cup vegetable oil
½ cup extra sharp
   Cheddar cheese,
   shredded
2 tablespoons onion,
   finely chopped

Brown sausage over medium heat, stirring to crumble. Drain well; set aside. In medium bowl, combine flour, baking powder, sugar, salt, thyme and cayenne pepper; make a well in center of mixture. Combine milk, egg and oil. Add to dry ingredients, stirring just until moistened. Stir in sausage, cheese and onion.

Place metal accessory rack on oven floor. Preheat oven to 350°F. Spoon batter into greased 1 ¾ x1-inch muffin pans, filling three-fourths full. Convection Bake at 350°F. for 15 to 18 minutes. Remove from pans immediately.

Total Convection Cooking Time 15 to 18 Minutes
Makes 5 dozen muffins

Barbecue Baby Back Ribs

2 lbs. baby back ribs, cut in
   serving size pieces
1 medium onion, chopped
2 cups hot tap water
Prepared Barbecue Sauce,
   page 85

In 3-quart casserole, place ribs, onion and water. Cover. Microwave at MEDIUM (5) 80 to 90 minutes, rearranging after 40 minutes. Drain. Pour prepared Barbecue Sauce over ribs. Cover. Microwave at HIGH (10) 5 to 8 minutes until heated through.

Total Microwave Cooking Time 1 hour 25 Minutes
to 1 hour 38 Minutes
Makes 6 servings

Sausage Crescents

⅓ cup onion, chopped
½ lb. lean bulk sausage
1 tablespoon catsup
½ teaspoon Italian seasoning
¼ teaspoon garlic powder
1 teaspoon fresh lemon juice
1 (8 oz.) pkg. crescent roll dough
1 egg, beaten

In 1-quart casserole, combine onion and sausage. Microwave at HIGH (10) 4 to 5 minutes, until sausage is thoroughly cooked and onion is tender; stir after 2 minutes to crumble sausage. Drain off fat. Stir in catsup, Italian seasoning, garlic powder and lemon juice. Set aside to allow to cool. Place metal accessory rack on floor of oven. Preheat oven to 375°F. Cut pastry into 4 rectangles. Divide sausage mixture into fourths. Spread sausage mixture down center of dough. Brush long edges of pastry with beaten egg and fold over to seal, enclosing sausage completely. Brush dough with beaten egg. Cut each length into 1-inch pieces. Arrange on well-greased baking sheet. Convection Bake 9 to 12 minutes.

Total Convection Cooking Time 9 to 12 Minutes
Makes 24 appetizers

Spread sausage mixture down the center of dough.

Artichoke Dip

1 (14 oz.) can artichoke hearts, drained and finely chopped
1 cup mayonnaise
1 cup grated Parmesan cheese
¼ teaspoon garlic salt
Paprika

In 8-inch square glass baking dish, mix chopped artichokes with mayonnaise, Parmesan cheese and garlic salt. Sprinkle with paprika. Microwave at HIGH (10) 4 to 5 minutes, until heated through; stir after 2 minutes.

TO COOK BY CONVECTION: Place metal accessory rack on floor of oven. Preheat oven to 350°F. Convection Bake 15 to 20 minutes until heated through and top is light brown.

Total Microwave Cooking Time 4 to 5 Minutes
Total Convection Cooking Time 15 to 20 Minutes
Makes 2 cups

Cut each roll into 1-inch slices and arrange on baking sheet.

Tiny Chicken Turnovers

½ (8 oz.) pkg. cream cheese, softened
½ cup butter, softened
1 cup all-purpose flour
1 cup cooked chicken, finely chopped
1 tablespoon onion, finely chopped
1 tablespoon sweet red pepper, finely chopped
2 tablespoons mayonnaise
1 teaspoon Dijon mustard
¼ teaspoon salt
⅛ teaspoon white pepper
1 egg, beaten

Beat cream cheese and butter together until light and fluffy. Blend in flour to make a soft dough. Turn out onto floured surface and knead lightly 10 to 12 strokes. Wrap in plastic wrap and refrigerate until firm enough to handle.

Combine chicken, onion, red pepper, mayonnaise, mustard, salt and pepper; blend thoroughly. Set aside while rolling out dough.

Roll dough on well-floured surface to 1/16-inch thickness. Cut into 3-inch rounds. Place one heaping teaspoon filling on each pastry round. Brush edges of pastry with egg. Fold pastry rounds in half over filling. Seal edges together with a fork. Brush tops with remaining egg. Place metal accessory rack on floor of oven. Preheat oven to 375°F. Convection Bake 13 to 16 minutes or until golden.

Total Convection Cooking Time 13 to 16 Minutes
Makes 20 appetizers

Appetizers & Beverages

Hot Cheese Dip

¼ cup onion, finely
　　chopped
1 tablespoon butter
1 teaspoon cornstarch
¼ teaspoon pepper
½ cup whipping cream
2 teaspoons Worcestershire
　　sauce
1 teaspoon soy sauce
2 cups American cheese,
　　shredded
1 (3 oz.) pkg. cream
　　cheese, softened
2 teaspoons parsley,
　　snipped
Assorted chips or vegetable
　　dippers

In 1½-quart casserole, combine onion and butter. Microwave at HIGH (10) 1 to 2 minutes until onion is tender. Blend in cornstarch, pepper, cream, Worcestershire sauce and soy sauce. Microwave at HIGH (10) 2 to 5 minutes, until slightly thickened and bubbly, stirring every minute. Add American cheese, cream cheese and parsley. Microwave at HIGH (10) 3 to 4 minutes, until cheese is melted and mixture is heated through, stirring every minute.

Beer Cheese Dip: Prepare Hot Cheese Dip as above, substituting ¾ cup beer for cream.

Chili con Queso Dip: Prepare Hot Cheese Dip as above, substituting 1 cup shredded Monterey Jack cheese for 1 cup American cheese. Add 4-oz. can mild chopped green chili peppers and ⅛ teaspoon hot sauce when cheeses are added. Before serving, stir in 1 medium tomato, peeled, seeded and finely chopped.

Total Microwave Cooking Time 6 to 11 Minutes
Makes 8 servings

Brie In Pastry

Wrap dough over cheese to completely enclose. Moisten edges with water to seal.

1 sheet (half of a 17¼ oz.
　　pkg.) puff pastry,
　　thawed and unfolded
1 (14 to 18 oz.) round of
　　Brie cheese
1 egg, beaten

Place metal accessory rack on floor of oven. Preheat oven to 375°F. Roll pastry to form a 12-inch square. Cut a 1-inch strip from each side of square. Roll 3 of the strips to 18-inch length and braid or twist to make 1 strip.

Place Brie, top down, in center of square of dough. Wrap dough over cheese, completely enclosing cheese. Moisten edges of dough with water and seal well. Place sealed-side down on cookie sheet. Moisten bottom edge of dough and gently press braid around side; press ends together to seal. Use remaining strip of dough to make decorative cutouts for top.

Using a pastry brush, brush egg over dough. Convection Bake 15 to 20 minutes until pastry is puffed and lightly browned. Let stand 20 minutes before serving.

Total Convection Cooking Time 15 to 20 Minutes
Makes 1 round

Gently press braid around side and press ends to seal.

Sugar Glazed Walnuts

½ cup butter, melted
1 cup brown sugar, packed
1 teaspoon cinnamon
1 lb. walnut halves
　　(about 4 cups)

In 1½-quart casserole, combine melted butter, brown sugar and cinnamon. Microwave at HIGH (10) 2 to 3 minutes; stir after 1 minute. Add nuts and mix to coat. Microwave at HIGH (10) 3 to 5 minutes. Spread onto wax paper and cool slightly. Refrigerate in airtight container.

Total Microwave Cooking Time 5 to 8 Minutes
Makes 1 pound

Hot Chocolate

⅔ cup sugar
½ cup water
4 (1 oz.) squares
   unsweetened chocolate,
   cut up
5 cups milk

In 2-quart casserole, combine sugar, water and chocolate. Microwave at HIGH (10) 1 to 2 minutes, until chocolate is melted; stir after 45 seconds with a wire whisk. Blend in milk. Microwave at HIGH (10) 6 to 9 minutes, until hot, stirring every 3 minutes.

Peppermint Hot Chocolate: Prepare Hot Chocolate as above; stir in 1 or 2 drops Peppermint Schnapps after melting the chocolate.

S'more Hot Chocolate: Prepare Hot Chocolate as above; stir in ⅓ cup marshmallow creme after melting the chocolate.

Irish Hot Chocolate: Prepare Hot Chocolate as above; stir in ⅓ cup Irish Creme Liqueur after melting the chocolate.

Total Microwave Cooking Time 7 to 11 Minutes
Makes 4 (6 oz.) servings

Vary the flavor of Hot Chocolate by adding marshmallow creme or a flavored liqueur.

Zippy Tomato Cocktail

1 (12 oz.) can vegetable
   juice cocktail
½ cup beef broth
1 tablespoon lemon juice
1 teaspoon Worcestershire
   sauce
¼ teaspoon prepared
   horseradish
2 drops hot sauce
¼ cup vodka (optional)
Celery sticks (optional)

In 4-cup glass measure, combine vegetable juice cocktail, beef broth, lemon juice, Worcestershire sauce, horseradish and hot sauce. Microwave at HIGH (10) 7 to 9 minutes, until hot; stir after 4 minutes. If desired, stir in vodka and serve with celery sticks.

Total Microwave Cooking Time 7 to 9 Minutes
Makes 2 (8 oz.) servings

Irish Coffee

2 to 3 cups strong coffee
4 teaspoons sugar
6 oz. Irish whiskey
Sweetened whipped cream

Pour ½ to ¾ cup coffee in each of 4 (10 to 12 oz.) cups. Microwave at HIGH (10) 3 to 4 minutes. For each drink, stir in 1 teaspoon sugar and 1½ ounces Irish whiskey; top with whipped cream.

Total Microwave Cooking Time 3 to 4 Minutes
Makes 4 servings

Hot Buttered Rum

4 cups apple juice
4 cinnamon sticks
4 tablespoons brown sugar,
   packed
4 oz. rum
4 teaspoons butter
Dash nutmeg

In each of 4 (10 to 12 oz.) mugs, combine 1 cup apple juice, 1 cinnamon stick and 1 tablespoon sugar. Microwave at HIGH (10) 3 to 4 minutes. For each drink stir in 1 oz. rum; top with 1 teaspoon butter and dash nutmeg.

Total Microwave Cooking Time 3 to 4 Minutes
Makes 4 servings

Soups & Stews

Minestrone Soup

1½ lbs. stew beef, cut into
 ½-inch cubes, fat and
 gristle removed
5 cups hot water
1 medium onion, chopped
1 clove garlic, minced
1 teaspoon basil
¼ teaspoon pepper
1 (14½ oz.) can tomatoes
2 bay leaves
2 cups pasta, one-inch
 in length, uncooked
1½ cups small zucchini,
 sliced ¼-inch thick
1 cup cabbage, finely
 shredded
1 (10 oz.) pkg. frozen
 green beans
½ cup celery, chopped
2 tablespoons fresh
 parsley, snipped
½ teaspoon salt
1 (10 oz.) pkg. frozen baby
 carrots
1 (16 oz.) can navy beans

In 3-quart casserole, place beef, water, onion, garlic, basil, pepper, tomatoes and bay leaves. Cover. Microwave at HIGH (10) 20 to 25 minutes until meat is tender. Add pasta, zucchini, cabbage, green beans, celery, parsley and salt. Cover. Microwave at HIGH (10) 14 to 17 minutes until vegetables and pasta are tender. Add baby carrots and navy beans. Cover. Microwave at HIGH (10) 10 to 12 minutes; stir after 5 minutes. Remove bay leaves. Cover and let stand 5 minutes before serving.

Total Microwave Cooking Time 44 to 54 Minutes
Makes 8 to 10 servings

Cheese Soup with Broccoli, Cauliflower and Sausage

2 tablespoons butter
½ lb. smoked beef sausage
 or kielbasa, cubed
1 medium onion, chopped
½ teaspoon caraway seed,
 crushed
Dash pepper
1 bay leaf
2 (14½ oz.) cans chicken
 broth
3 medium potatoes, peeled
 and sliced
1½ cups broccoli flowerets
1½ cups cauliflower
 flowerets
¼ cup milk
1½ cups sharp Cheddar
 cheese, shredded

In 2-quart casserole, place butter, sausage, onion, caraway seed, pepper and bay leaf. Microwave at HIGH (10) 4 to 6 minutes, until sausage begins to brown and onion is tender, stirring every 2 minutes. Add chicken broth, potatoes, broccoli and cauliflower. Microwave at MEDIUM HIGH (7) 28 to 32 minutes, until vegetables are tender, stirring every 7 minutes. Stir in milk and Microwave at HIGH (10) 4 to 6 minutes until heated through. Discard bay leaf. Add cheese and stir until completely melted. Serve immediately.

Total Microwave Cooking Time 36 to 44 Minutes
Makes 2 to 4 servings

Soups & Stews

▲ *Beef Stew*

Beef Stew

3 slices bacon, diced
1 small onion, sliced
1 clove garlic, minced
1 ½ cups water
1 (1 ¾ oz.) pkg. dry onion soup mix
1 teaspoon thyme
¾ teaspoon oregano
½ teaspoon pepper
2 lbs. boneless beef chuck, cut into ½ -inch cubes
½ lb. fresh mushrooms, sliced
2 large potatoes, peeled and cut into ½ -inch cubes
½ cup celery, sliced ½ -inch thick
3 tablespoons cornstarch
½ cup water
1 (10 oz.) pkg. frozen cut green beans
1 (10 oz.) pkg. frozen baby carrots

In 3-quart casserole, place bacon, onion and garlic. Cover. Microwave at HIGH (10) 7 to 9 minutes; stir after 3 minutes. Add 1 ½ cups water, onion soup mix, thyme, oregano and pepper. Add meat and stir to coat. Cover. Microwave at MEDIUM HIGH (7) 30 minutes; stir after 15 minutes. Add mushrooms, potatoes and celery. Cover. Microwave at MEDIUM HIGH (7) 30 minutes, until meat and vegetables are tender, stirring every 10 minutes.

In 2-cup measure, combine cornstarch with ½ cup water, stirring to blend well. Add cornstarch mixture, green beans and carrots to stew; stir until blended. Cover. Microwave at HIGH (10) 7 to 10 minutes; stir after 3 minutes.

Total Microwave Cooking Time 1 hour 14 Minutes to 1 hour 19 Minutes
Makes 6 to 8 servings

Cheddar Broccoli Soup

2 lbs. broccoli, chopped
2 tablespoons butter
½ cup onions, chopped
¼ cup green pepper,
   chopped
1 bay leaf
2 tablespoons fresh
   parsley, chopped
¼ teaspoon salt
1 teaspoon thyme
6 black peppercorns
⅛ teaspoon nutmeg
2 (14½ oz.) cans chicken
   broth
4 tablespoons all-purpose
   flour
3 egg yolks, beaten
1 cup milk
1 cup sharp Cheddar
   cheese, shredded

In 3-quart casserole, combine broccoli, butter, onions, green pepper, bay leaf, parsley, salt, thyme, peppercorns and nutmeg. Cover. Microwave at HIGH (10) 8 to 10 minutes, until broccoli is tender; stir after 4 minutes. Remove bay leaf. Spoon mixture into blender. Add 1 can chicken broth. Blend for 1 minute on low speed.

Blend flour and remaining broth in 3-quart casserole. Stir well using a wire whisk. Add broccoli mixture; stir to blend. Microwave at HIGH (10) 10 to 12 minutes; stir after 5 minutes.

In 1-quart casserole, blend eggs and milk. Gradually add egg mixture to soup, stirring constantly. Add cheese. Microwave at HIGH (10) 4 minutes, until cheese is completely melted, stirring after 2 minutes.

Total Microwave Cooking Time 22 to 26 Minutes
Makes 4 to 6 servings

Combine cooked vegetables and seasonings in a blender.

Burgundy Beef Stew

4 slices bacon, diced
1 large onion, chopped
2 medium carrots, sliced
   ¼-inch thick
3 cloves garlic, finely
   chopped
1½ cups Burgundy wine
¼ cup brandy
1½ teaspoons thyme
1 teaspoon oregano
1 teaspoon salt
½ teaspoon pepper
3 lbs. boneless beef chuck,
   cut into 1-inch cubes
1 (8 oz.) pkg. frozen small
   whole onions
½ lb. fresh mushrooms,
   quartered
¼ cup water
¼ cup all-purpose flour

In 3-quart casserole, place bacon, onions, carrots and garlic. Cover. Microwave at HIGH (10) 5 to 7 minutes, until bacon is cooked and vegetables are tender; stir after 3 minutes. Blend in wine, brandy, thyme, oregano, salt and pepper. Add meat and stir to coat. Microwave at MEDIUM (5) 29 to 31 minutes. Add onions and mushrooms. Microwave at MEDIUM (5) 15 to 20 minutes, until meat and vegetables are tender, stirring every 5 minutes.

In 1-cup measure blend water and flour to make a smooth paste. Stir into stew. Cover. Microwave at HIGH (10) 5 to 7 minutes; stir after 3 minutes. Serve over noodles, if desired.

Total Microwave Cooking Time 54 to 65 Minutes
Makes 8 to 10 servings

Soups & Stews

Cheesy Vegetable Soup

1 cup water
1 large potato, shredded
1 small onion, finely
  chopped
3 small carrots, grated
1 stalk celery, finely
  chopped
1 cup chicken broth
½ cup half & half
1½ cups sharp Cheddar
  cheese, shredded
Dash salt
Dash white pepper

In 2-quart casserole, combine water, potato, onion, carrots and celery. Cover. Microwave at HIGH (10) 10 to 12 minutes, until potatoes are tender; stir after 5 minutes. Blend in chicken broth and half & half. Cover. Microwave at MEDIUM HIGH (7) 6 to 8 minutes, until heated through. Add cheese, salt and pepper; stir until cheese is completely melted.

**Total Microwave Cooking Time 16 to 20 Minutes
Makes 4 servings**

Creamy Mushroom Soup

Coarsely chop stems and add to broth for flavor.

2 lbs. fresh mushrooms
2 (14 ½ oz.) cans chicken
  broth
1 (1 ¾ oz.) pkg. dry onion
  soup mix
3 tablespoons butter, sliced
3 tablespoons all-purpose
  flour
1 cup half & half
3 egg yolks
¼ cup sherry
Dash hot sauce or pinch
  cayenne
Dash pepper

Thinly slice mushroom caps and set aside. Coarsely chop stems and place in 4-cup glass measure. Add 1 can of chicken broth. Microwave at HIGH (10) 10 minutes until broth is brown. Strain broth into 3-quart casserole; discard mushroom pieces. Add soup mix, remaining chicken broth, mushroom caps and butter. Microwave at HIGH (10) 15 to 18 minutes, uncovered; stir after 7 minutes. In 4-cup glass measure, combine flour, half & half and egg yolks; whisk until smooth. Gradually add cream mixture, sherry, hot sauce and pepper to hot soup, stirring constantly with a wire whisk. Microwave at HIGH (10) 8 to 10 minutes, until slightly thickened, stirring every 4 minutes.

**Total Microwave Cooking Time 33 to 38 Minutes
Makes 6 to 8 servings**

Chicken Noodle Soup

Strain broth and discard mushroom pieces before adding the soup mix.

2 lbs. chicken pieces
4 celery stalks, cut up
2 bay leaves
2 teaspoons peppercorns
1 teaspoon salt
1 onion, sliced
6 cups hot water
3 carrots, shredded
1 to 1½ cups egg noodles,
  uncooked

In 3-quart casserole, combine chicken, celery, bay leaves, peppercorns, salt, onion and water. Cover. Microwave at HIGH (10) 10 minutes. Stir. Continue to Microwave at MEDIUM (5) 35 to 37 minutes until chicken is tender. Strain chicken from broth. Return broth to casserole and set chicken aside to cool. Add carrots and noodles to broth. Remove chicken from bone, coarsely chop and add to broth. Cover. Microwave at MEDIUM HIGH (7) 7 to 8 minutes until noodles and carrots are tender. Remove and discard bay leaves.

**Total Microwave Cooking Time 52 to 55 Minutes
Makes 8 servings**

Chili

1 lb. ground chuck
1 medium onion, chopped
½ cup green pepper,
   chopped
1 (14 ½ oz.) can whole
   tomatoes, chopped
1 (15 ½ oz.) can kidney
   beans, undrained
1 (6 oz.) can tomato paste
½ cup water
1 teaspoon garlic salt
1 teaspoon chili powder
1 teaspoon oregano
½ teaspoon ground cumin
Dash hot sauce
½ teaspoon cayenne pepper

In 2-quart casserole, combine ground chuck, onion and green pepper. Cover. Microwave at HIGH (10) 4 to 6 minutes, until meat is browned, stirring every 2 minutes. Drain. Add tomatoes, kidney beans, tomato paste, water, garlic salt, chili powder, oregano, ground cumin, hot sauce and cayenne pepper; stir to blend. Cover. Microwave at MEDIUM HIGH (7) 20 to 25 minutes, stirring every 7 minutes. Let stand, covered, for 5 minutes before serving.

Total Microwave Cooking Time 24 to 31 Minutes
Makes 4 to 6 servings

French Onion Soup

¼ cup butter
4 medium onions, thinly
   sliced
3 cloves garlic, minced
2 (13 ¾ oz.) cans beef broth
2 tablespoons dry sherry
½ teaspoon salt
⅛ teaspoon fresh ground
   pepper
4 to 5 slices French bread
1 to 1 ½ cups Swiss cheese,
   shredded

In 3-quart casserole, place butter, onions and garlic. Microwave at HIGH (10) 5 to 8 minutes until onions are tender. Add beef broth, sherry, salt and pepper; stir to blend. Microwave at HIGH (10) 10 to 12 minutes.

Top individual servings of soup with one slice of French bread; sprinkle with Swiss cheese. Microwave at HIGH (10) 30 to 45 seconds until cheese is completely melted.

Total Microwave Cooking Time 15½ to 20¾ Minutes
Makes 4 to 5 servings

Add cheese for topping and microwave.

Clam Chowder

1 tablespoon bacon
   drippings
2 tablespoons onion, diced
1 small potato, peeled and
   cubed
½ cup water
½ teaspoon seasoned salt
Dash pepper
1 tablespoon all-purpose
   flour
1 cup milk, divided
1 (6 ½ oz.) can minced
   clams, undrained
1 tablespoon butter

In 2-quart casserole, combine bacon drippings and onion. Microwave at HIGH (10) 2 to 3 minutes until onion is tender. Add potatoes, water, seasoned salt and pepper. Cover. Microwave at HIGH (10) 5 to 6 minutes, until potatoes are tender; stir after 2 minutes. Add flour to ¼ cup milk; stir well to blend. Add flour mixture, remaining ¾ cup milk, clams and butter to potatoes and onions. Microwave at HIGH (10) 6 to 8 minutes, stirring every 2 minutes.

Total Microwave Cooking Time 13 to 17 Minutes
Makes 3 servings

Meats

Flank Steak Florentine

1½ to 1¾ lb. beef flank
   steak
½ cup fresh mushrooms,
   chopped
1 medium onion, chopped
1 small carrot,
   finely chopped
1 clove garlic, minced
3 tablespoons butter
1 (10 oz.) pkg. frozen
   chopped spinach,
   thawed and well drained
2 teaspoons instant beef
   bouillon granules
¼ cup hot water
1 (10¾ oz.) can cream of
   chicken soup
2 tablespoons capers,
   drained
2 tablespoons dry
   vermouth, optional
½ teaspoon curry powder
¼ teaspoon coriander
¼ teaspoon white pepper

Pound flank steak with a wooden mallet to ⅛-inch thickness; score with a sharp knife. In 1½-quart casserole, combine mushrooms, onion, carrot, garlic, butter and spinach. Cover. Microwave at HIGH (10) 2 to 3 minutes. Spread spinach mixture over steak. Starting at long side, roll steak in jelly roll fashion. Tie with string or secure with toothpicks.

Place steak, seam side up, in 2-quart oblong glass baking dish. In 4-cup glass measure, dissolve bouillon granules in hot water. Add soup, capers, vermouth, curry powder, coriander and pepper. Pour over steak; cover. Place metal accessory rack on floor of oven. Preheat oven to 325°F. Cook on Combination 70 to 80 minutes until tender; turn meat over after 40 minutes.

TO COOK BY MICROWAVE: Cover with vented plastic wrap. Microwave at HIGH (10) 10 minutes. Microwave at LOW (3) 40 to 45 minutes; turn steak over after 20 minutes. Let stand, covered, 10 minutes.

> Total Combination Cooking Time 70 to 80 Minutes
> Total Microwave Cooking Time 50 to 55 Minutes
> Makes 4 servings

Barbecued Beef Brisket

1 cup catsup
2 tablespoons
   Worcestershire sauce
1 tablespoon Dijon
   mustard
1 tablespoon red wine
   vinegar
1 tablespoon brown sugar
½ teaspoon salt
¼ teaspoon garlic salt
¼ teaspoon celery salt
⅛ teaspoon cayenne
   pepper
1 (3 to 4 lb.) beef brisket

In small bowl, combine catsup, Worcestershire sauce, mustard, vinegar, sugar, salt, garlic salt, celery salt and cayenne pepper. Pierce brisket on both sides with a fork. Place in 2-quart oblong glass baking dish. Pour half of sauce over brisket; cover.

Microwave at HIGH (10) 15 minutes. Microwave at MEDIUM (5) 45 minutes. Turn over and add remaining sauce. Cover. Microwave at MEDIUM (5) 45 to 50 minutes until tender. Let stand, covered, 10 minutes.

TO COOK BY COMBINATION: Place metal accessory rack on floor of oven. Preheat oven to 300°F. Cook on Combination 1½ to 2 hours; turn meat over and add remaining sauce after 1 hour.

> Total Microwave Cooking Time 1 Hour 45 Minutes
> to 1 Hour 50 Minutes
> Total Combination Cooking Time 1½ to 2 Hours
> Makes 6 to 8 servings

Meats

▲ *Beef Rib Eye Roast with Mushroom Sauce*

Beef Rib Eye Roast with Mushroom Sauce

¼ cup bourbon
1 cup water
1 tablespoon lemon juice
1 tablespoon steak sauce
½ teaspoon garlic salt
½ teaspoon lemon-pepper seasoning
¼ teaspoon cayenne pepper
1 (4 to 5 lb.) beef rib eye roast
½ lb. fresh mushrooms, sliced
½ cup water
2 teaspoons instant beef bouillon granules
2 teaspoons browning sauce
2 tablespoons cornstarch
¼ cup water

In 4-cup glass measure, combine bourbon, 1 cup water, lemon juice, steak sauce, garlic salt, lemon-pepper and cayenne pepper. Pierce roast with a fork in several places. Place meat in 2-quart oblong glass baking dish. Pour marinade over roast and cover. Marinate in refrigerator 8 hours, turning occasionally. Drain and reserve ½ cup marinade.

Place metal accessory rack on floor of oven. Place roast on trivet in 2-quart oblong glass baking dish. Cook on Combination to desired doneness according to directions in chart, page 137.

Mushroom Sauce: In 1½-quart casserole, combine reserved marinade, mushrooms, ½ cup water, bouillon granules and browning sauce. Microwave at HIGH (10) 2 to 3 minutes. Combine cornstarch and ¼ cup water; stir into mushroom mixture. Microwave at HIGH (10) 2 to 3 minutes, until thickened, stirring every minute.

Makes 10 to 12 servings

Cheese-Stuffed Meat Loaf

1 ½ cups soft
   bread crumbs
1 egg, slightly beaten
½ teaspoon seasoned salt
¼ teaspoon pepper
½ cup milk
¾ cup onion, chopped,
   divided
1 ½ lbs. ground chuck
2 tablespoons green
   pepper, chopped
2 tablespoons celery,
   chopped
1 (2 oz.) jar sliced
   pimento, drained
1 tablespoon lemon juice
1 egg, slightly beaten
1 cup Cheddar cheese,
   shredded
½ cup soft bread crumbs

In large mixing bowl, combine 1 ½ cups bread crumbs, 1 egg, seasoned salt, pepper, milk, ½ cup chopped onion and ground chuck.

In 1 ½-quart casserole, combine ¼ cup chopped onion, green pepper, celery, pimento and lemon juice. Microwave at HIGH (10) 2 to 3 minutes until crisp-tender. Add egg; blend well. Stir in cheese and ½ cup bread crumbs.

On strip of wax paper, shape meat mixture into a 14x7-inch rectangle. Spread cheese mixture over meat. Lifting wax paper for support, roll meat mixture from short side in jelly roll fashion. Place seam-side down in 9x5-inch glass loaf dish. Cover with vented plastic wrap. Microwave at MEDIUM HIGH (7) 23 to 26 minutes. Add topping (see below) and Microwave, uncovered, at MEDIUM HIGH (7) 4 to 5 minutes. Let stand 5 minutes.

Spicy Tomato Topping: In small bowl, combine ¾ cup catsup, ¼ cup brown sugar, ¾ teaspoon dry mustard, ¼ teaspoon allspice and ⅛ teaspoon cloves.

TO COOK BY COMBINATION: Place metal accessory rack on floor of oven. Do not cover meat loaf. Preheat oven to 350°F. Cook on Combination 35 to 40 minutes. Add topping and cook on Combination an additional 5 minutes.

Total Microwave Cooking Time 29 to 34 Minutes
Total Combination Cooking Time 40 to 45 Minutes
Makes 6 servings

Spread cheese mixture over meat within ½-inch from sides.

Carefully roll up meat mixture from the short side to form roll.

Marinated Pot Roast

1 (3 to 4 lb.) boneless
   chuck roast
1 teaspoon pepper
½ teaspoon salt
¼ teaspoon garlic powder
¾ cup zesty Italian salad
   dressing
1 (10 oz.) pkg. frozen
   baby carrots
½ lb. fresh mushrooms,
   sliced
1 (6 oz.) can tomato paste

Pierce roast on both sides with a fork. Place in 3-quart casserole. Combine pepper, salt and garlic powder; sprinkle over roast. Pour salad dressing over roast. Cover and refrigerate 6 to 8 hours, turning twice.

Microwave at HIGH (10) 15 minutes. Microwave at MEDIUM (5) 55 to 60 minutes; turn roast over after 25 minutes. Add carrots and mushrooms. Cover and Microwave at MEDIUM (5) 9 to 11 minutes. Remove meat and vegetables to warm platter. Add tomato paste to cooking liquid; stir well. Microwave at HIGH (10) 3 to 4 minutes. Serve with meat and vegetables.

Total Microwave Cooking Time 1 Hour 19 Minutes
to 1 Hour 26 Minutes
Makes 6 servings

Pierce roast with a fork to allow seasonings to penetrate before marinating.

Meats

Scandinavian Meatballs

For evenly shaped meatballs, use an ice cream scoop to divide meat mixture.

1 lb. ground chuck
½ lb. ground veal
½ lb. ground pork
2 cups soft bread crumbs
½ cup milk
1 egg
1 (1¾ oz.) pkg. dry onion
    soup mix
½ teaspoon pepper
¼ teaspoon nutmeg
⅛ teaspoon allspice
1 teaspoon instant beef
    bouillon granules
1 cup hot water
3 tablespoons all-purpose
    flour
1 cup half & half

Mix together ground meats, bread crumbs, milk, egg, onion soup mix, pepper, nutmeg and allspice. Shape into 24 meatballs. Place meatballs in 3-quart oblong glass baking dish. Cover with wax paper. Microwave at HIGH (10) 11 to 14 minutes, rearranging meatballs after 6 minutes. Remove meatballs to warm platter. Reserve ¼ cup drippings and return to dish.

Dissolve bouillon granules in hot water. Add flour to reserved drippings; stir until smooth. Gradually stir in bouillon and half & half. Microwave at HIGH (10) 4 to 5 minutes, until thickened, stirring every 2 minutes. Return meatballs to dish; turn over to coat evenly. Microwave at HIGH (10) 2 to 3 minutes until hot. Serve over noodles.

Total Microwave Cooking Time 17 to 22 Minutes
Makes 8 servings

Savory Swiss Steak

1½ lb. boneless round
    steak, pounded
    ¼-inch thick
1 (14½ oz.) can whole
    tomatoes, chopped
1 (8 oz.) can tomato sauce
1 (1¾ oz.) pkg. dry onion-
    mushroom soup mix
2 tablespoons fresh
    parsley, snipped
1 teaspoon basil
¼ teaspoon oregano
¼ teaspoon garlic powder

Cut steak into serving size portions. In 3-quart casserole, combine steak, tomatoes, tomato sauce, soup mix, parsley, basil, oregano and garlic powder. Cover. Microwave at HIGH (10) 4 to 5 minutes and at MEDIUM (5) 35 to 40 minutes. Let stand, covered, 5 minutes before serving.

TO COOK BY COMBINATION: Place metal accessory rack on floor of oven. Preheat oven to 325°F. Cook on Combination 65 to 70 minutes. Let stand, covered, 5 minutes before serving.

Total Microwave Cooking Time 39 to 45 Minutes
Total Combination Cooking Time 65 to 70 Minutes
Makes 4 to 6 servings

Taco Salad

1½ lbs. ground chuck
½ cup onion, chopped
1 cup green pepper,
    chopped
1 (16 oz.) can hot chili
    beans in chili gravy
1 (10 oz.) can mild
    enchilada sauce
1 (8 oz.) can tomato sauce
1 (8 oz.) can mild
    taco sauce
1 (10 oz.) pkg. corn chips
1 cup Cheddar cheese,
    shredded
4 cups lettuce, shredded
2 cups tomatoes, chopped

In 1½-quart casserole, crumble beef. Add onion and green pepper; cover. Microwave at HIGH (10) 5 to 6 minutes; stir after 3 minutes. Drain well. Add chili beans. Cover. Microwave at HIGH (10) 5 to 6 minutes until hot. Set aside and keep warm.

In 2-quart casserole, combine enchilada sauce, tomato sauce and taco sauce. Microwave at HIGH (10) 4 to 6 minutes; stir after 3 minutes.

In large salad bowl, layer corn chips, meat mixture, half of cheese, lettuce and tomatoes. Top with sauce and sprinkle with remaining cheese. Serve immediately.

Total Microwave Cooking Time 14 to 18 Minutes
Makes 6 to 8 servings

▲ *Stuffed Peppers*

Stuffed Peppers

4 medium yellow,
    green or red peppers
1 lb. ground chuck beef
½ cup onion, chopped
⅓ cup celery, chopped
1 clove garlic, minced
1 (7 ½ oz.) can tomatoes
⅔ cup cooked rice
1 (2 oz.) jar sliced
    pimento, drained
¼ teaspoon pepper
1 (10 ¾ oz.) can tomato
    soup
½ teaspoon basil
¼ cup sharp Cheddar
    cheese, shredded

Cut off tops of peppers. Remove seeds and membrane; set aside. In 1 ½-quart casserole, crumble beef. Add onion, celery and garlic. Microwave at HIGH (10) 5 to 7 minutes; stir after 3 minutes. Drain well. Combine meat mixture, tomatoes, rice, pimento and pepper. Fill peppers with meat mixture. Place peppers in a 2-quart casserole. Combine soup and basil; pour over peppers. Cover. Microwave at HIGH (10) 16 to 19 minutes. Sprinkle cheese over peppers. Let stand, covered, 5 minutes.

TO COOK BY COMBINATION: Place metal accessory rack on floor of oven. Preheat oven to 375°F. Cook on Combination 27 to 30 minutes. Sprinkle with cheese before serving.

Total Microwave Cooking Time 21 to 26 Minutes
Total Combination Cooking Time 27 to 30 Minutes
Makes 4 servings

Oriental Beef and Vegetables

1 lb. boneless top sirloin
    steak
1 clove garlic, minced
3 tablespoons soy sauce
3 tablespoons dry sherry
1 tablespoon cornstarch
1 teaspoon brown sugar
¼ teaspoon ginger
2 teaspoons vegetable oil
1 (6 oz.) pkg. frozen pea
    pods, thawed
1 medium sweet red
    pepper, cut into strips
1 (8 oz.) can sliced water
    chestnuts, drained

Slice steak diagonally across grain into 2 ½ x ½-inch strips. In medium bowl, combine garlic, soy sauce, sherry, cornstarch, brown sugar and ginger. Add beef, mix well and refrigerate 30 minutes. Drain, reserving marinade.

Place beef and oil in 2-quart oblong glass baking dish. Cover with wax paper. Microwave at HIGH (10) 8 to 10 minutes, until beef is no longer pink; stir after 5 minutes. Add reserved marinade, pea pods, red pepper and water chestnuts. Cover. Microwave at HIGH (10) 7 to 9 minutes until sauce is thickened and vegetables are crisp-tender; stir after 4 minutes.

Tuck wax paper under ends of dish to hold securely in place.

Total Microwave Cooking Time 15 to 19 Minutes
Makes 4 to 6 servings

Meats

▲ *Glazed Pork Roast with Pineapple Salsa*

Glazed Pork Roast with Pineapple Salsa

1 large pineapple, peeled, cored & finely chopped
1 small sweet red pepper, finely chopped
1 small green pepper, finely chopped
1 small red onion, finely chopped
3 tablespoons fresh parsley, snipped
2 tablespoons fresh chives, snipped
2 tablespoons lemon juice
1 tablespoon vegetable oil
¼ teaspoon cayenne pepper
⅛ teaspoon white pepper
1 (4 to 5 lb.) pork loin roast

Combine pineapple, green and red pepper, onion, parsley, chives, lemon juice, oil, cayenne pepper and white pepper. Cover and refrigerate 2 hours.

Place metal accessory rack on floor of oven. Preheat oven to 325°F. Place roast on trivet in 2-quart oblong glass baking dish. Cook pork roast according to directions in chart, pages 136 or 137. During last 5 minutes of cooking time, baste roast occasionally with Pineapple Glaze (see below). Serve with salsa.

Pineapple Glaze: Combine ½ cup pineapple preserves, 1 tablespoon orange juice, ¼ teaspoon cinnamon and ⅛ teaspoon ginger.

Makes 6 to 8 servings

Classic Ham Loaf

1 lb. ground cooked ham
½ lb. ground fresh pork
½ cup soft bread crumbs
½ cup water
1 egg
½ cup onion, finely chopped
¼ teaspoon pepper
¼ teaspoon marjoram

Combine all ingredients. Place in 9x5-inch glass loaf dish. Cover with vented plastic wrap. Microwave at MEDIUM HIGH (7) 24 to 28 minutes. Let stand 5 minutes before serving.

TO COOK BY COMBINATION: Place metal accessory rack on floor of oven. Preheat oven to 350°F. Do not cover dish. Cook on Combination 30 to 35 minutes. Let stand 5 minutes.

Total Microwave Cooking Time 24 to 28 Minutes
Total Combination Cooking Time 30 to 35 Minutes
Makes 6 servings

Italian Sloppy Joes

1½ lbs. mild bulk
   Italian sausage
½ cup onion, chopped
½ cup green pepper,
   chopped
1 (2.2 oz.) can sliced ripe
   olives, drained
1 (28 oz.) can whole
   tomatoes, drained and
   chopped
½ teaspoon oregano
¼ teaspoon salt
⅛ teaspoon garlic powder
¼ teaspoon pepper
3 hamburger buns, split
   and toasted
½ cup mozzarella cheese,
   shredded

In 2-quart casserole, crumble sausage. Add onion and green pepper. Microwave at HIGH (10) 8 to 10 minutes; stir after 4 minutes. Drain well. Add olives, tomatoes, oregano, salt, garlic powder and pepper. Microwave at HIGH (10) 4 to 6 minutes until hot.

Serve over split, toasted hamburger buns. Sprinkle with mozzarella cheese.

Total Microwave Cooking Time 12 to 16 Minutes
Makes 6 servings

When microwaving sausage, use a microwave-safe colander inside the casserole dish to eliminate draining.

Sweet and Sour Ham

1 (20 oz.) can pineapple
   chunks
1 (10½ oz.) can beef broth
3 tablespoons cornstarch
2 cups cooked ham,
   cut into 1-inch cubes
1 small green pepper,
   cut into strips
1 small sweet red pepper,
   cut into strips
1 small onion,
   thinly sliced
¾ teaspoon dry mustard
2 tablespoons brown sugar
3 tablespoons vinegar

Drain pineapple, reserving ⅓ cup juice. In 3-quart casserole, combine reserved juice, beef broth and corn-starch; stir until smooth. Microwave at HIGH (10) 4 to 5 minutes, until thickened; stir after 2 minutes.

Add pineapple chunks, ham, green and red pepper, onion, dry mustard, brown sugar and vinegar. Micro-wave at HIGH (10) 5 to 6 minutes until vegetables are crisp-tender. Serve over Chinese noodles or rice.

Total Microwave Cooking Time 9 to 11 Minutes
Makes 4 servings

Lemon Pork Chops

4 center-cut pork chops,
   ¾-inch thick
½ teaspoon salt
¼ teaspoon pepper
⅛ teaspoon thyme
4 onion slices
4 lemon slices
½ cup chili sauce
1 tablespoon brown sugar

Sprinkle chops with salt, pepper and thyme. Arrange chops in 3-quart casserole. Combine chili sauce and brown sugar; pour over chops. Place onion and lemon slice on each chop. Cover. Place metal accessory rack on floor of oven. Preheat oven to 350°F. Cook on Combination 35 to 40 minutes until tender.

TO COOK BY MICROWAVE: Microwave at MEDIUM HIGH (7) 25 to 30 minutes until tender.

Total Combination Cooking Time 35 to 40 Minutes
Total Microwave Cooking Time 25 to 30 Minutes
Makes 4 servings

Meats

Barbecued Spareribs

2 ½ to 3 lbs. pork
    spareribs, cut into
    2-rib pieces
1 medium onion, chopped
1 medium sweet red
    pepper, chopped
2 cloves garlic, minced
½ cup catsup
½ cup brown sugar
¼ cup molasses
2 tablespoons lemon juice
1 teaspoon prepared
    brown mustard
Dash hot sauce

Place ribs in 3-quart casserole; cover. Microwave at MEDIUM (5) 30 minutes. In small mixing bowl, combine onion, red pepper, garlic, catsup, sugar, molasses, lemon juice, mustard and hot sauce. Turn ribs over and add sauce. Cover and Microwave at MEDIUM (5) 40 to 45 minutes. Let stand 5 minutes.

TO COOK BY COMBINATION: Place metal accessory rack on floor of oven. Preheat oven to 350°F. Cook on Combination 1 to 1 ¼ hours; baste with sauce during last 30 minutes.

Total Microwave Cooking Time 1 Hour 10 Minutes to 1 Hour 15 Minutes
Total Combination Cooking Time 1 to 1 ¼ Hours
Makes 4 servings

Fruited Pork Tenderloin

2 to 3 (2 ½ to 3 lbs. total)
    whole pork tenderloins
¼ cup butter, melted
1 cup Madeira wine
1 tablespoon molasses
¼ teaspoon garlic powder
2 teaspoons thyme
1 cup pitted prunes
1 cup dried apricots

Place tenderloins in 3-quart oblong glass baking dish. In small bowl, combine butter, wine, molasses, garlic powder and thyme. Pour over tenderloins. Cover and marinate in refrigerator 6 to 8 hours or overnight.

Place metal accessory rack on floor of oven. Preheat oven to 350°F. Cook on Combination 30 minutes. Turn tenderloins over and add prunes and apricots, making certain that fruit is submerged in liquid. Continue cooking on Combination 30 to 35 minutes. Let stand 5 minutes.

TO COOK BY CONVECTION: Place metal accessory rack on floor of oven. Preheat oven to 325°F. Bake for 1 ¼ to 1 ½ hours; add fruit during last 30 minutes of cooking time.

Total Combination Cooking Time 60 to 65 Minutes
Total Convection Cooking Time 75 to 90 Minutes
Makes 6 servings

Peachy Glazed Ham Slice

1 (8 ¾ oz.) can peach
    slices, drained
2 tablespoons honey
2 tablespoons lemon juice
¼ teaspoon ground
    allspice
1 teaspoon grated
    lemon rind
1 (1 ¼ -inch thick) fully
    cooked center
    ham slice

In a blender container, combine peach slices, honey, lemon juice and allspice. Cover and blend until smooth; stir in lemon rind.

Place ham in 1 ½ -quart oblong glass baking dish. Cover with wax paper. Microwave at HIGH (10) 6 to 7 minutes. Uncover, brush with glaze and continue Microwaving at HIGH (10) 2 to 3 minutes. Pour remaining glaze in 2-cup glass measure. Microwave at HIGH (10) 1 to 2 minutes or until heated through. Spoon glaze over ham.

Total Microwave Cooking Time 9 to 12 Minutes
Makes 6 to 8 servings

▲ *Apple-Stuffed Pork Chops*

Apple-Stuffed Pork Chops

1 cup herb-seasoned
  stuffing mix
⅔ cup apple, diced
¼ cup onion,
  finely chopped
3 tablespoons raisins
¼ cup orange juice
2 tablespoons butter,
  melted
1 tablespoon grated
  orange rind
½ teaspoon salt
¼ teaspoon cinnamon
¼ teaspoon allspice
4 center-cut pork chops,
  1-inch thick
½ cup currant jelly
2 tablespoons orange juice

In mixing bowl, combine stuffing mix, apple, onion, raisins, ¼ cup orange juice, butter, orange rind, salt, cinnamon and allspice. Cut a pocket in each pork chop. Divide stuffing evenly among chops.

Arrange chops in 2-quart oblong glass baking dish with thickest meaty areas to outside edges. In 1-cup glass measure, combine currant jelly and 2 tablespoons orange juice. Microwave at HIGH (10) 1 to 2 minutes; stir well. Brush half of mixture over chops.

Place metal accessory rack on floor of oven. Preheat oven to 375°F. Cook on Combination 33 to 38 minutes; rotate dish ½ turn after 20 minutes. Spoon remaining jelly mixture over chops before serving.

TO COOK BY MICROWAVE: Cover with wax paper. Microwave at MEDIUM HIGH (7) 25 to 30 minutes; rotate dish ½ turn after 15 minutes.

Total Combination Cooking Time 33 to 38 Minutes
Total Microwave Cooking Time 26 to 32 Minutes
Makes 4 servings

To form a pocket, use a sharp knife to cut pork chop through center.

Place the stuffing in pocket.

Meats

▲ *Veal Roll-Ups*

Tasty Veal Chops

**6 veal loin chops,
  ¾ -inch thick**
¼ cup water
¼ cup dry sherry
2 tablespoons soy sauce
¼ teaspoon marjoram
¼ teaspoon pepper
½ cup water
2 tablespoons cornstarch
**1 (4 oz.) can sliced
  mushrooms, drained**
**1 (8 oz.) can sliced water
  chestnuts, drained**

Place chops in 3-quart casserole. Combine ¼ cup water, sherry, soy sauce, marjoram and pepper; pour over chops. Cover and let stand at room temperature 1 hour; turn once. Microwave at MEDIUM HIGH (7) 19 to 23 minutes until tender; turn over after 10 minutes. Remove chops to warm platter.

Combine ½ cup water and cornstarch; stir until smooth. Add to cooking liquid. Microwave at HIGH (10) 2 to 3 minutes, until thickened, stirring every minute. Add mushrooms and water chestnuts. Microwave at HIGH (10) 2 to 3 minutes until hot. Spoon sauce over chops.

TO COOK BY COMBINATION: Place metal accessory rack on floor of oven. Preheat oven to 350°F. Cook on Combination 27 to 30 minutes. Microwave sauce as described above.

Total Microwave Cooking Time 23 to 29 Minutes
Total Combination Cooking Time 27 to 30 Minutes
Makes 6 servings

Veal Roll-Ups

6 boneless veal cutlets,
 ½-inch thick
6 thin slices Swiss cheese
6 thin slices boiled ham
2 eggs
¼ cup butter, melted
½ cup dry bread crumbs
¼ cup all-purpose flour
1 teaspoon salt
½ teaspoon paprika
¼ teaspoon onion powder
¼ teaspoon sage
¼ teaspoon pepper

Pound each cutlet with wooden mallet to ¼-inch thickness. Place 1 slice cheese and 1 slice ham on each piece of veal. Roll up firmly and fasten with a toothpick.

In small bowl, beat together eggs and butter. In shallow dish, combine bread crumbs, flour, salt, paprika, onion powder, sage and pepper. Dip veal rolls in egg mixture, then roll in crumb mixture. Place rolls in 2-quart oblong glass baking dish. Place metal accessory rack on floor of oven. Preheat oven to 325°F. Cook on Combination 20 to 25 minutes.

Total Combination Cooking Time 20 to 25 Minutes
Makes 4 to 6 servings

Place cheese and ham on top of flattened veal cutlet.

Veal with Rosemary

1½ lbs. veal round steak,
 cut into strips
2 tablespoons butter
1 (4 oz.) jar sliced
 mushrooms, undrained
2 green onions, sliced
1 teaspoon rosemary
½ teaspoon salt
¼ teaspoon pepper
1 tablespoon cornstarch
¼ cup water
2 tomatoes, cut in wedges
2 tablespoons fresh
 parsley, snipped

Place veal, butter, mushrooms, onions, rosemary, salt and pepper in 2-quart casserole; cover. Microwave at MEDIUM HIGH (7) 20 minutes. Combine cornstarch and water; stir until smooth. Add to veal mixture. Microwave at HIGH (10) 2 to 3 minutes, until thickened; stir after 1 minute. Add tomatoes and parsley and Microwave at HIGH (10) 2 minutes until hot. Serve over noodles or rice.

Total Microwave Cooking Time 24 to 25 Minutes
Makes 6 servings

Dip veal roll in egg mixture then roll in crumb mixture.

Leg of Lamb with Mustard Glaze

½ cup Dijon mustard
1 teaspoon basil
¼ teaspoon thyme
¼ teaspoon white pepper
2 tablespoons vegetable oil
2 tablespoons
 Worcestershire sauce
1 (4 to 5 lb.) leg of lamb

Combine mustard, basil, thyme, pepper, oil and Worcestershire sauce. Pierce lamb in several places with fork. Place fat side up on trivet in 3-quart oblong glass baking dish. Spread mustard mixture over lamb. Chill 2 hours.

TO COOK BY COMBINATION: Place metal accessory rack on floor of oven. Preheat oven to 325°F. Cook on Combination to desired doneness according to chart on page 137.

TO COOK BY CONVECTION: Place metal accessory rack on floor of oven. Preheat oven to 325°F. Convection Bake to desired doneness according to chart on page 136.

Makes 6 to 8 servings

Meats

▲ *Zesty Lamb Kabobs*

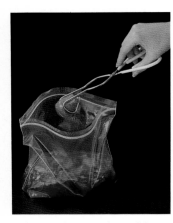

Self sealing bags may be used for marinating meats and vegetables, but are not recommended for microwaving.

Zesty Lamb Kabobs

1 ⅓ cups dry red wine
2 tablespoons vegetable oil
1 cup onion,
   finely chopped
2 cloves garlic, crushed
2 tablespoons Dijon
   mustard
1 bay leaf
½ teaspoon salt
½ teaspoon pepper
½ teaspoon thyme
¼ teaspoon ginger
2 lbs. lamb, cut in 1-inch
   cubes
2 large green peppers,
   cut in 1-inch squares
2 large red peppers,
   cut in 1-inch squares
3 medium onions,
   cut in eighths
3 tablespoons cornstarch
Cooked rice

In 2-quart casserole, combine wine, oil, onion, garlic, mustard, bay leaf, salt, pepper, thyme and ginger. Add lamb cubes. Cover and marinate in refrigerator several hours or overnight. Remove lamb from marinade. Reserve marinade.

On 8-inch wooden skewers, thread red or green pepper square, onion chunk and lamb cube. Repeat, ending with onion chunk and pepper square. Place 4 kabobs on microwave-safe plate. Microwave at HIGH (10) 4 to 5 minutes. Repeat with remaining kabobs. Place kabobs on a bed of cooked rice and keep warm.

In 4-cup glass measure, combine reserved marinade and cornstarch; stir until smooth. Microwave at HIGH (10) 4 to 5 minutes, until thickened, stirring every 2 minutes. Remove bay leaf. Pour sauce over kabobs before serving.

Total Microwave Cooking Time 12 to 15 Minutes
Makes 4 servings

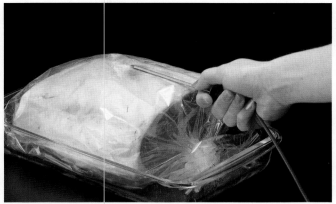

TO INSERT PROBE: Measure the distance to the center of the roast by laying the temperature probe on top of the meat. Mark with your thumb and forefinger where the edge of the meat comes on the probe.

Insert probe from top of roast at a slight angle up to the point marked by your finger. Make sure that tip of probe reaches the center of the meat. **NOTE: For best results, place roast in cooking bag following manufacturer's instructions.**

Meat Roasting Chart for Microwave Cooking

MEAT		Power Level	Approximate Cooking Time	Internal Temperature
Beef	**Rib, Boneless Rib, Top Sirloin***			
	Rare	Medium (5)	8 to 11 min./lb.	140°F.
	Medium	Medium (5)	11 to 14 min./lb.	160°F.
	Well	Medium (5)	14 to 17 min./lb.	170°F.
	Standing Rib, high quality, bone-in roast*			
	Rare	Medium (5)	8 to 11 min./lb.	140°F.
	Medium	Medium (5)	11 to 14 min./lb.	160°F.
	Well	Medium (5)	14 to 17 min./lb.	170°F.
	Pot Roast* (2 ½ to 3 ½ lbs.)			
	Chuck	Low (3)	20 to 23 min./lb.	
	Oblong glass baking dish with cooking bag			
	Rump	Low (3)	20 to 23 min./lb.	
	3-quart casserole with lid.			
	*Turn meat over after ½ of cooking time. For best results, use a cooking bag.			
Pork	**Bone-in***	Medium (5)	14 to 17 min./lb.	170°F.
	Boneless*	Medium (5)	14 to 17 min./lb.	170°F.
	Pork Chops* (½ to 1-inch thick)			
	2 chops	Medium (5)	15 to 18 min. total	
	4 chops	Medium (5)	18 to 21 min. total	
	6 chops	Medium (5)	21 to 24 min. total	
	*Turn over and rearrange (if appropriate) after ½ of cooking time. Use a cooking bag for roasts.			
Ham	**Canned* (3 lbs.)**	Medium (5)	13 to 15 min./lb.	140°F.
	Butt* (3 to 4 lbs.)	Medium (5)	13 to 15 min./lb.	140°F.
	Shank* (3 to 4 lbs.)	Medium (5)	13 to 15 min./lb.	140°F.
	*Turn over after ½ of cooking time. (Cooking bag may be used.)			
Lamb	**Bone-in***			
	Medium	Medium (5)	13 to 17 min./lb.	170°F.
	Well	Medium (5)	18 to 22 min./lb.	180°F.
	Boneless*			
	Medium	Medium (5)	18 to 22 min./lb.	170°F.
	Well	Medium (5)	24 to 28 min./lb.	180°F.
	Lamb Chops* (½ to 1-inch thick)			
	2 chops	Medium High (7)	7 to 10 min. total	
	4 chops	Medium High (7)	9 to 11 min. total	
	6 chops	Medium High (7)	12 to 14 min. total	
	*Turn over and rearrange (if appropriate) after ½ cooking time. Cooking bag may be used.			

Poultry

Oriental Chicken and Cashews

3 tablespoons oil, heated
2 (1 to 1¼ lb.) boneless
   chicken breasts,
   skinned & thinly sliced
2 cloves garlic, minced
2 tablespoons soy sauce
1 tablespoon sherry
1 tablespoon cornstarch
¼ teaspoon ginger
1 medium green pepper,
   cut into small chunks
½ cup cashews

In 2-quart oblong glass baking dish, combine oil, chicken, garlic, soy sauce, sherry, cornstarch and ginger. Microwave at HIGH (10) 3 to 4 minutes, stirring every minute. Add green pepper and cashews. Cover with plastic wrap. Microwave at HIGH (10) 2 to 3 minutes, until chicken is done and green pepper is tender; stir after 1 minute. Let stand 3 minutes before serving. Serve over rice.

Total Microwave Cooking Time 5 to 7 Minutes
Makes 4 servings

Turkey with Vegetables

2 tablespoons butter
¼ lb. fresh mushrooms,
   sliced
¼ cup carrots,
   thinly sliced
¼ cup celery, sliced
1 lb. cooked turkey,
   thinly sliced
¼ cup white wine
¼ cup chicken broth
⅛ teaspoon pepper
¼ teaspoon salt
1½ teaspoons cornstarch
1 tablespoon parsley,
   snipped

In 2-quart casserole, combine butter, mushrooms, carrots and celery. Microwave at HIGH (10) 3 to 4 minutes. Add turkey slices and Microwave at HIGH (10) 5 to 6 minutes until turkey is heated through. Combine wine, broth, pepper, salt, cornstarch and parsley; pour over turkey. Stir to coat. Microwave at HIGH (10) 2 to 3 minutes, stirring every minute.

Total Microwave Cooking Time 10 to 13 Minutes
Makes 4 servings

Sweet and Tangy Chicken

1 (2½ to 3½ lb.) chicken,
   cut up
2 tablespoons mayonnaise
1 (1¾ oz.) pkg. dry onion
   soup mix
1 cup bottled Russian
   dressing
1 cup apricot-pineapple
   preserves

Place metal accessory rack on floor of oven. Preheat oven to 375°F. Arrange chicken in 2-quart oblong glass baking dish, with thickest meaty pieces to outside edges. In small mixing bowl, combine mayonnaise, onion soup mix, dressing and preserves. Pour over chicken. Cook on Combination 38 to 43 minutes.

TO COOK BY CONVECTION: Place metal accessory rack on floor of oven. Preheat oven to 375°F. Convection Bake 45 to 50 minutes.

Total Combination Cooking Time 38 to 43 Minutes
Total Convection Cooking Time 45 to 50 Minutes
Makes 4 servings

Poultry

▲ *Turkey Curry*

Turkey Curry

3 tablespoons butter
½ cup onion, chopped
1 medium apple, peeled and coarsely chopped
¼ cup raisins
3 tablespoons all-purpose flour
1 teaspoon curry powder
½ teaspoon coriander
¼ teaspoon cumin
¼ teaspoon ginger
1 cup half & half
1 cup hot water
1 teaspoon instant chicken bouillon granules
3 cups cooked turkey, chopped

In 2-quart casserole, place butter, onion, apple and raisins. Microwave at HIGH (10) 3 to 4 minutes. Add flour, curry powder, coriander, cumin and ginger; stir until smooth. Gradually stir in half & half, water and bouillon. Microwave at HIGH (10) 4 to 6 minutes, until thickened, stirring every 2 minutes. Add turkey and Microwave at HIGH (10) 1 to 2 minutes until heated through. Serve over rice.

Total Microwave Cooking Time 8 to 12 Minutes
Makes 6 servings

Roast Duck with Orange Sauce

1 (4 to 5 lb.) duck
¼ cup butter, melted
2 tablespoons cider
    vinegar
2 tablespoons sugar
1 cup chicken broth
2 tablespoons cornstarch
1 tablespoon orange peel,
    grated
½ cup orange juice
1 teaspoon lemon juice

Tuck wing tips under back of duck. Brush with melted butter. Place breast side down on trivet in 2-quart oblong glass baking dish. Set aside.

In 1½-quart casserole, combine vinegar and sugar. Microwave at HIGH (10) 2 minutes, until lightly browned; stir after 1 minute. Add broth, cornstarch, orange peel, orange juice and lemon juice. Microwave at HIGH (10) 4 to 6 minutes, until clear and thickened, stirring every 2 minutes. Baste duck with orange sauce. Place metal accessory rack on floor of oven. Preheat oven to 375°F. Cook on Combination 1 hour, basting duck every 20 minutes. Turn breast side up after 30 minutes.

Total Combination Cooking Time 1 Hour
Makes 6 servings

Pierce skin of breast and legs to release fat after turning duck over.

Hot Chicken Salad

1½ cups cooked chicken,
    diced
½ cup celery,
    finely chopped
½ cup slivered almonds,
    toasted
½ cup butter cracker
    crumbs
¼ cup onion, chopped
1 (10¾ oz.) can cream of
    chicken soup
½ cup mayonnaise
¼ teaspoon salt
¾ cup Cheddar cheese,
    shredded

Place metal accessory rack on floor of oven. Preheat oven to 350°F. In 1½-quart casserole, combine chicken, celery, almonds, cracker crumbs, onion, chicken soup, mayonnaise and salt. Mix well. Cook on Combination 15 to 20 minutes. Sprinkle cheese over top and continue to cook 5 minutes until cheese melts.

Total Combination Cooking Time 20 to 25 Minutes
Makes 4 servings

Chicken Parmesan

¾ cup seasoned dry
    bread crumbs
¼ cup grated Parmesan
    cheese
¼ teaspoon paprika
1 egg, beaten
¼ cup water
2 (1 to 1¼ lb.) boneless
    chicken breasts, skinned,
    split and pounded thin
1 cup spaghetti sauce
1 cup mozzarella cheese,
    shredded

Place metal accessory rack on floor of oven. Preheat oven to 375°F. In small mixing bowl, combine bread crumbs, Parmesan cheese and paprika. Set aside. In shallow dish, blend egg and water together. Dip chicken breast in egg mixture and then in bread crumb mixture. In 3-quart oblong glass baking dish, arrange chicken. Pour spaghetti sauce over top and sprinkle with mozzarella cheese. Convection Bake 22 to 26 minutes.

Total Convection Cooking Time 22 to 26 Minutes
Makes 4 servings

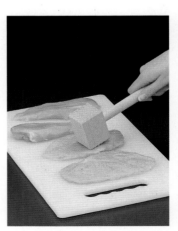

Pound chicken breast to ¼-inch thickness.

Poultry

Press crescent roll perforations together to seal.

Top with chicken and ⅓ cup spinach mixture.

Fold dough over chicken to form a triangle and seal edges.

Crescent-Wrapped Curried Chicken Breasts

**2 cups water
4 boneless chicken breast
    halves, skinned
4 teaspoons curry powder
1 (10 oz.) pkg. frozen
    chopped spinach,
    thawed and drained
1 (8 oz.) container
    sour cream
1 (3 oz.) pkg. cream cheese
1 teaspoon coriander
2 (8 oz.) pkgs.
    crescent rolls
1 cup Swiss cheese,
    shredded, divided**

Butter Sauce:
**½ cup butter
1 tablespoon lemon juice
¼ teaspoon pepper
¼ teaspoon dry mustard
3 egg yolks, beaten**

In 3-quart casserole, place water, chicken and curry. Microwave at MEDIUM HIGH (7) 8 to 10 minutes; stir after 5 minutes. Drain and set aside. Place metal accessory rack on floor of oven. Preheat oven to 350°F. In medium mixing bowl, combine spinach, sour cream, cream cheese and coriander. Divide each package of crescent rolls in half. Press perforations together to seal. On each square place, ¼ cup Swiss cheese, one chicken breast and ⅓ cup spinach mixture. Fold dough in half over chicken to form triangles; press edges to seal. Place on ungreased 15x10-inch aluminum baking sheet. Convection Bake 20 to 25 minutes until golden brown.

> **Total Convection Cooking Time 20 to 25 Minutes**
> **Makes 4 servings**

In 2-cup glass measure, place butter, lemon juice, pepper and mustard. Microwave at HIGH (10) 1 minute until butter melts. With a wire whisk, blend in egg yolks. Microwave at MEDIUM (5) 30 seconds to 1 minute. Pour over chicken.

> **Total Microwave Cooking Time**
> **1 Minute 30 Seconds to 2 Minutes**

Creamy Chicken Delight

**1 cup celery, chopped
¼ cup water
3 (5 oz.) cans cooked
    chicken chunks
1 cup rice, cooked
1 (10 ¾ oz.) can cream of
    chicken soup
2 tablespoons onion,
    chopped
¾ cup mayonnaise
1 (8 oz.) can
    water chestnuts,
    drained and sliced
½ cup slivered almonds
¼ teaspoon pepper
¼ teaspoon celery seed
¼ teaspoon garlic powder
½ teaspoon basil
2 teaspoons parsley flakes
2 tablespoons butter
½ cup bread crumbs**

In 4-cup glass measure, combine celery and water. Cover with plastic wrap and Microwave at HIGH (10) 2 to 3 minutes. Drain.

Place metal accessory rack on floor of oven. Preheat oven to 350°F. In greased 3-quart casserole, combine celery, chicken, rice, soup, onion, mayonnaise, water chestnuts, almonds, pepper, celery seed, garlic powder, basil and parsley flakes. Dot with butter and sprinkle with bread crumbs. Cook on Combination 30 to 35 minutes.

TO COOK BY CONVECTION: Place metal accessory rack on floor of oven. Preheat oven to 350°F. Convection Bake 35 to 40 minutes.

> **Total Combination Cooking Time 30 to 35 Minutes**
> **Total Convection Cooking Time 35 to 40 Minutes**
> **Makes 6 to 8 servings**

▲ *Teriyaki Cornish Hens*

Teriyaki Cornish Hens

1 ½ tablespoons
  cornstarch
3 tablespoons brown sugar
¼ teaspoon dry mustard
⅛ teaspoon ginger
½ cup teriyaki sauce
¼ cup orange juice
4 (1 to 1½ lb.) Cornish
  hens
1 (6 oz.) pkg. long grain
  and wild rice mix,
  cooked
½ cup dried apricots,
  finely chopped

In 1-quart casserole, combine cornstarch, brown sugar, dry mustard and ginger. Blend in teriyaki sauce and orange juice; stir until smooth. Microwave at HIGH (10) 3 to 4 minutes, until thickened, stirring every minute.

Place metal accessory rack on floor of oven. Preheat oven to 375°F. Remove giblets from hens; rinse with cold water and pat dry. In small mixing bowl, combine rice and apricots. Stuff hens with rice mixture and close cavities. Secure with toothpicks. In 3-quart oblong glass baking dish, place hens, breast side up, on trivet. Cook on Combination 55 minutes to 1 hour 5 minutes, basting with teriyaki sauce during last 15 minutes.

Total Combination Cooking Time 55 Minutes to
1 Hour 5 Minutes
Makes 4 servings

Poultry

▲ *Mint-Laced Chicken*

Mint-Laced Chicken

Place fresh mint leaves in cavity of chicken.

1 (3 to 3 ½ lb.)
   whole chicken
½ teaspoon salt
¼ teaspoon garlic powder
¼ teaspoon lemon pepper
1 cup fresh mint leaves
¼ cup butter, melted
2 tablespoons lemon juice

Place metal accessory rack on floor of oven. Preheat oven to 375°F. Rinse chicken with cold water and pat dry. Combine salt, garlic powder and lemon pepper. Sprinkle inside chicken cavity. Place mint leaves in cavity of chicken.

Combine butter and lemon juice; brush over outside of chicken. Place chicken, breast side up on trivet in 2-quart oblong glass baking dish. Cook on Combination 45 to 50 minutes until done.

Total Combination Cooking Time 45 to 50 Minutes
Makes 4 to 6 servings

Hawaiian Turkey

1 cup fresh snow peas
¼ cup water
1 small onion, thinly
   sliced
¼ cup green pepper,
   chopped
1 stalk celery, sliced
   diagonally
2 cups cooked turkey,
   cubed
1 (15 ½ oz.) can pineapple
   chunks, reserve juice
5 teaspoons cornstarch
2 teaspoons instant
   chicken bouillon
   granules
Dash ground ginger
1 tablespoon brown sugar
3 tablespoons soy sauce
2 tablespoons vinegar

Place snow peas and water in 3-quart casserole. Microwave at HIGH (10) 2 to 4 minutes. Drain. Add onion, green pepper, celery, turkey and pineapple chunks.

In 4-cup glass measure, combine pineapple juice, cornstarch, bouillon, ginger, brown sugar, soy sauce and vinegar. Microwave at HIGH (10) 2 to 4 minutes until sauce is clear and thickened, strring every minute. Pour sauce over turkey and vegetables; stir to coat. Cover. Microwave at HIGH (10) 6 to 8 minutes until heated through.

Total Microwave Cooking Time 10 to 16 Minutes
Makes 4 servings

Chicken A La Roma

2 tablespoons olive oil
¾ cup green onions,
 thinly sliced
2 cloves garlic, minced
½ lb. fresh mushrooms,
 sliced
1 (6 oz.) can tomato paste
1 (8 oz.) can tomato sauce
½ cup dry white wine
1 tablespoon instant
 chicken bouillon
 granules
1 teaspoon basil
2 teaspoons parsley flakes
1 teaspoon oregano
½ cup ripe olives, sliced
¼ teaspoon pepper
1 (2½ to 3 lb.) chicken,
 cut up
1 (6 oz.) jar marinated
 artichoke hearts,
 drained
¼ cup grated Parmesan
 cheese

In 8-inch square baking dish, place oil, onion, garlic and mushrooms. Cover with wax paper. Microwave at HIGH (10) 4 to 6 minutes. Drain.

In 4-cup glass measure, combine tomato paste, tomato sauce, white wine, bouillon, basil, parsley, oregano, olives and pepper. Add onion, garlic and mushroom mixture.

Place chicken pieces in 3-quart casserole. Add tomato mixture. Cover. Microwave at HIGH (10) 10 minutes; rotate ½ turn. Microwave at MEDIUM HIGH (7) 16 to 18 minutes. Arrange artichoke hearts around chicken pieces and sprinkle with Parmesan cheese. Cover. Microwave at HIGH (10) 4 to 5 minutes. Let stand 5 minutes before serving.

TO COOK BY COMBINATION: Place metal accessory rack on floor of oven. Preheat oven to 375°F. Cook on Combination 50 minutes. Arrange artichoke hearts around chicken and top with Parmesan cheese. Cook on Combination 5 to 10 minutes.

> Total Microwave Cooking Time 34 to 39 Minutes
> Total Combination Cooking Time 55 to 60 Minutes
> Makes 4 to 6 servings

Chicken Italiano

2 tablespoons olive oil
½ lb. fresh mushrooms,
 sliced
½ cup onion, chopped
2 cloves garlic, minced
6 boneless chicken breast
 halves, skinned
⅔ cup dry white wine
¾ teaspoon Italian herb
 seasoning
¼ teaspoon basil
1 cup spaghetti sauce
¼ cup grated Parmesan
 cheese
¼ teaspoon red pepper
 flakes

In 3-quart casserole, place oil, mushrooms, onion and garlic. Microwave at HIGH (10) 2 to 4 minutes until tender. Add chicken. Microwave at HIGH (10) 6 to 8 minutes. Turn over. Add wine, Italian seasoning and basil. Microwave at MEDIUM (5) 5 to 8 minutes.

Place metal accessory rack on floor of oven. Preheat oven to 350°F. Spread spaghetti sauce over chicken. Sprinkle with Parmesan cheese and red pepper flakes. Convection Bake 20 to 30 minutes.

> Total Convection Cooking Time 20 to 30 Minutes
> Makes 4 servings

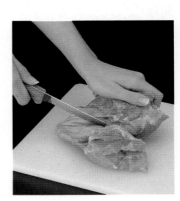

To bone chicken breast, split the breast in half lengthwise.

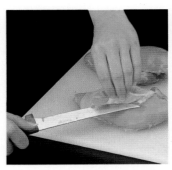

Starting at the breast bone side of the chicken, slice meat away from the bone.

Poultry

▲ *Chicken Cacciatore*

Chicken Cacciatore

1 (2 ½ to 3 lb.) chicken, cut up
1 medium green pepper, coarsely chopped
1 medium onion, sliced
1 large tomato, seeded and coarsely chopped
1 (15 oz.) can tomato sauce
1 (6 oz.) can tomato paste
¼ cup dry red wine
1 bay leaf
½ teaspoon oregano
¼ teaspoon fennel seed
¼ teaspoon pepper
½ cup grated Parmesan cheese
Capellini or spaghetti, optional

In 3-quart casserole, place chicken pieces with meaty portions along outside of dish. Add green pepper and onion slices.

In 4-cup glass measure, combine tomato, tomato sauce, tomato paste, wine, bay leaf, garlic, oregano, fennel seed and pepper. Mix well and pour over chicken. Cover. Microwave at HIGH (10) 20 to 25 minutes until chicken is done and vegetables are tender; rotate dish ½ turn after 10 minutes. Remove bay leaf. Sprinkle with Parmesan cheese. Serve over capellini or spaghetti.

Total Microwave Cooking Time 20 to 25 Minutes
Makes 6 servings

Chicken In Pastry Shells

1 tablespoon butter
1 cup fresh mushrooms,
    sliced
½ cup green pepper,
    chopped
2 tablespoons butter,
    melted
3 tablespoons all-purpose
    flour
½ cup chicken broth
½ cup milk
2 tablespoons dry sherry
½ teaspoon salt
¼ teaspoon pepper
2 (5 oz.) cans cooked
    chicken
6 pastry shells, baked

In 2-quart casserole, place 1 tablespoon butter, mushrooms and green pepper. Microwave at HIGH (10) 4 to 5 minutes, until mushrooms are tender; stir after 2 minutes. Drain.

In 4-cup glass measure, combine remaining butter and flour. Gradually add broth and milk, stirring constantly until smooth. Microwave at HIGH (10) 3 to 4 minutes, until thickened, stirring every minute. Add mushrooms, green pepper, sherry, salt, pepper and chicken. Microwave at HIGH (10) 6 to 8 minutes until heated through. Serve in baked pastry shells.

**Total Microwave Cooking Time 13 to 17 Minutes
Makes 6 servings**

Remove the center of pastry shells before filling.

Chicken Gumbo

1 (2 ½ to 3 lb.) chicken,
    cut up
1 lb. smoked sausage,
    cut into ¼-inch slices
¼ cup vegetable oil
2 cups onion, chopped
1 small green pepper,
    chopped
1 small red pepper,
    chopped
¼ cup all-purpose flour
3 cups water
2 chicken-flavored
    bouillon cubes
½ teaspoon pepper

In 3-quart casserole, place chicken, sausage and oil. Microwave at HIGH (10) 10 to 12 minutes; turn chicken over after 5 minutes. In small mixing bowl, combine onion, green pepper and red pepper. Microwave at HIGH (10) 6 to 7 minutes until tender. Add to chicken.

In 4-cup glass measure, combine flour and water; stir until blended. Microwave at HIGH (10) 3 to 5 minutes; stir after 2 minutes. Add bouillon and pepper; mix well and pour over chicken and vegetables. Place metal accessory rack on floor of oven. Preheat oven to 350°F. Cook on Combination 35 to 40 minutes. Serve over rice.

**Total Combination Cooking Time 35 to 40 Minutes
Makes 4 to 6 servings**

Curried Chicken and Rice

2 tablespoons butter
6 boneless chicken breast
    halves, skinned and
    cut into ½-inch cubes
1 medium onion, chopped
2 (10 ¾ oz.) cans cream of
    chicken soup
¼ cup fresh parsley,
    snipped
1 tablespoon curry powder
¼ teaspoon seasoned salt
⅛ teaspoon pepper
3 cups cooked rice

In 3-quart casserole, place butter, chicken and onion. Microwave at HIGH (10) 7 to 8 minutes, until chicken is no longer pink, stirring every 2 minutes. Add chicken soup, parsley, curry, seasoned salt, pepper and rice. Place metal accessory rack on floor of oven. Preheat oven to 350°F. Convection Bake 25 to 30 minutes.

**Total Convection Cooking Time 25 to 30 Minutes
Makes 6 servings**

Poultry

Chicken Normandy

3 tablespoons butter
2 large apples, sliced
1 cup celery, sliced
3 tablespoons cornstarch
¼ cup apple juice
½ cup sweet and sour
    sauce
1 cup chicken broth
¼ cup whipping cream
2 tablespoons apple brandy
½ teaspoon salt
¼ teaspoon pepper
6 boneless chicken breast
    halves, skinned

In 3-quart oblong glass baking dish, place butter, apples and celery. Microwave at HIGH (10) 5 to 6 minutes. In medium mixing bowl, combine cornstarch, apple juice, sweet and sour sauce, chicken broth, whipping cream and apple brandy. Pour over apples. Microwave at HIGH (10) 8 to 9 minutes, stirring every 3 minutes. Add salt and pepper. Arrange chicken breasts over apples. Cover with vented plastic wrap. Microwave at HIGH (10) 12 to 15 minutes until chicken is thoroughly cooked.

**Total Microwave Cooking Time 25 to 30 Minutes
Makes 4 to 6 servings**

Chicken & Peppers in White Wine Sauce

½ lb. bacon, cut into
    ¾-inch pieces
1 (3 lb.) chicken, cut up
1 large onion,
    coarsely chopped
1 large green pepper,
    coarsely chopped
1 large red pepper,
    coarsely chopped
1 teaspoon sage
¼ teaspoon ground thyme
¼ teaspoon salt
¼ teaspoon pepper
½ cup black olives, sliced
1 cup dry white wine

In 3-quart casserole, place bacon and Microwave at HIGH (10) 2 to 3 minutes. Place chicken in casserole, skin side down. Microwave at HIGH (10) 7 to 9 minutes; turn over chicken after 4 minutes and drain off fat. Add onion, green pepper, red pepper, sage, thyme, salt, pepper and olives. Stir. Pour wine over chicken. Cover. Microwave at HIGH (10) 8 to 11 minutes; stir. Microwave at MEDIUM HIGH (7) 8 to 11 minutes.

**Total Microwave Cooking Time 25 to 34 Minutes
Makes 6 servings**

Rice and Chicken Livers

Prick livers with toothpick prior to cooking to prevent bursting.

1 cup long grain rice
2⅓ cups chicken broth
½ teaspoon seasoned salt
1 bay leaf
3 tablespoons fresh
    parsley, snipped
2 stalks celery, chopped
⅛ teaspoon thyme
½ cup butter
½ cup onion, chopped
½ lb. fresh mushrooms,
    sliced
1 lb. chicken livers
¼ cup grated Parmesan
    cheese

In 2-quart casserole, combine rice, chicken broth, seasoned salt, bay leaf, parsley, celery and thyme. Microwave at HIGH (10) 15 minutes; stir. Microwave at MEDIUM HIGH (7) 10 to 15 minutes until rice is tender. Discard bay leaf.

In 3-quart casserole, combine butter, onion and mushrooms. Microwave at HIGH (10) 6 to 8 minutes; stir after 3 minutes. Prick chicken livers with toothpick to prevent bursting. Add chicken livers to onion-mushroom mixture and Microwave at HIGH (10) 8 to 10 minutes, stirring every 3 minutes. Add rice mixture; stir well. Sprinkle with Parmesan cheese. Place metal accessory rack on floor of oven. Preheat oven to 350°F. Convection Bake 20 to 30 minutes.

**Total Convection Cooking Time 20 to 30 Minutes
Makes 4 to 6 servings**

▲ *Chicken with Spicy Cheddar Sauce*

Chicken with Spicy Cheddar Sauce

½ cup cornflake crumbs
½ teaspoon paprika
¼ teaspoon garlic powder
4 boneless chicken breast halves, skinned
½ cup cheese spread with jalapeno peppers
¼ cup pitted ripe olives, sliced
1 (2 oz.) jar sliced pimento, drained and chopped

In medium mixing bowl, combine cornflake crumbs, paprika and garlic powder. Rinse chicken in water, then coat with crumb mixture. In 2-quart oblong glass baking dish, arrange chicken with meaty portions toward the edges of the dish. Cover. Microwave at HIGH (10) 15 to 18 minutes, until thoroughly cooked; rotate dish ½ turn after 6 minutes. Transfer chicken to platter and keep warm.

In 2-cup glass measure, combine cheese spread, olives and pimento. Microwave at HIGH (10) 1 minute until heated through. Pour sauce over chicken.

Total Microwave Cooking Time 16 to 19 Minutes
Makes 4 servings

Sauteed Chicken Livers with Wine Sauce

2 tablespoons onion, minced
1 clove garlic, minced
3 tablespoons butter
2 tablespoons all-purpose flour
1 cup beef broth
3 tablespoons dry red wine
¼ cup all-purpose flour
¼ teaspoon pepper
⅛ teaspoon garlic powder
1 lb. chicken livers
2 tablespoons butter, melted
1 (6 oz.) pkg. long grain and wild rice, cooked

In 1½-quart casserole, combine onions, garlic and butter. Microwave at HIGH (10) 2 to 3 minutes until onions are transparent. Add 2 tablespoons flour; stir until smooth. Gradually add beef broth and Microwave at HIGH (10) 2 to 3 minutes, until thickened, stirring every minute. Blend in wine and set aside.

In small mixing bowl, combine remaining flour, pepper and garlic powder. Coat chicken livers with flour mixture. Prick chicken livers to prevent bursting. In 2-quart casserole, place 2 tablespoons melted butter and chicken livers. Microwave at HIGH (10) 6 to 8 minutes, turning livers every 2 minutes. Add wine sauce to chicken livers and mix well. Microwave at HIGH (10) 3 to 4 minutes until heated through. Serve over rice.

Total Microwave Cooking Time 13 to 18 Minutes
Makes 4 servings

Poultry

Turkey Tetrazzini

¼ cup butter, melted
¼ cup all-purpose flour
1 cup chicken broth
1 cup half & half
4 cups cooked turkey,
  cut up
1 (2 oz.) jar pimento,
  chopped
1 (7 oz.) pkg. spaghetti,
  cooked and drained
1 (4 oz.) can sliced
  mushrooms, drained
½ teaspoon salt
½ teaspoon pepper
¼ cup grated Parmesan
  cheese

In 3-quart casserole, combine butter and flour. Gradually add broth and half & half, stirring until smooth. Microwave at MEDIUM HIGH (7) 5 to 6 minutes, until thickened, stirring every 2 minutes. Add turkey, pimento, spaghetti, mushrooms, salt and pepper. Sprinkle Parmesan cheese over top. Place metal accessory rack on floor of oven. Preheat oven to 350°F. Cook on Combination 25 to 30 minutes.

Total Combination Cooking Time 25 to 30 Minutes
Makes 6 servings

Chicken and Vegetables

½ cup all-purpose flour
¼ teaspoon seasoned salt
⅛ teaspoon pepper
1 (3 lb.) chicken, cut-up
3 tablespoons vegetable oil
1 small green pepper,
  thinly sliced
1 small red pepper,
  thinly sliced
2 cloves garlic, minced
3 medium tomatoes,
  peeled and chopped
1 cup fresh mushrooms,
  sliced
1 medium zucchini,
  thinly sliced
½ teaspoon salt
⅛ teaspoon pepper
⅛ teaspoon ground cumin
1½ cups hot water

In a plastic bag, combine flour, seasoned salt and pepper. Add chicken pieces and shake to coat. In 3-quart casserole, place chicken and vegetable oil. Microwave at HIGH (10) 6 to 7 minutes. Remove chicken from casserole and set aside. Add green pepper, red pepper and garlic. Microwave at HIGH (10) 4 to 5 minutes until tender; stir after 3 minutes. Add tomatoes, mushrooms, zucchini, salt, pepper, cumin and water. Return chicken pieces to casserole. Place metal accessory rack on floor of oven. Preheat oven to 350°F. Convection Bake 40 to 45 minutes until chicken is tender. Serve over rice.

Total Convection Cooking Time 40 to 45 Minutes
Makes 6 servings

Baked Chicken Bites

1½ cups bread crumbs
½ cup grated Parmesan
  cheese
½ teaspoon lemon pepper
½ teaspoon salt
1 tablespoon whole thyme
1 tablespoon basil
¾ cup butter, melted
½ teaspoon hot sauce
6 whole boneless chicken
  breasts, cubed

Place metal accessory rack on floor of oven. Preheat oven to 400°F. In 2-quart casserole, combine bread crumbs, Parmesan cheese, lemon pepper, salt, thyme and basil. Mix well. In small mixing bowl, combine butter and hot sauce. Dip chicken pieces in butter and coat with bread crumb mixture. Place coated chicken pieces in 15x10x1-inch jelly roll pan. Convection Bake 20 to 30 minutes until chicken is golden brown.

Total Convection Cooking Time 20 to 30 Minutes
Makes 8 to 10 servings

Place coated chicken pieces in jelly roll pan.

Hot Brown

Cheese Sauce:
2 tablespoons butter,
  melted
¼ cup all-purpose flour
1½ cups milk
¼ teaspoon salt
½ teaspoon white pepper
¾ cup sharp Cheddar
  cheese, shredded

6 slices bread, toasted
¾ lb. turkey, thinly sliced
12 bacon strips, cooked
6 slices tomato
¼ cup grated Parmesan
  cheese

In 4-cup glass measure, combine butter and flour. Stir until smooth. Gradually add milk, salt, pepper and Cheddar cheese. Microwave at HIGH (10) 4 to 5 minutes, stirring every minute.

Place metal accessory rack on floor of oven. Preheat oven to 400°F. Place toast on 15x10x1-inch jelly roll pan. Arrange turkey slices on toast and cover with hot cheese sauce. Convection Bake 10 to 12 minutes until heated through. Top with bacon strips and tomato slices. Sprinkle with Parmesan cheese.

Total Convection Cooking Time 10 to 12 Minutes
Makes 6 servings

Spicy Marinated Chicken

2 cloves garlic, crushed
3 tablespoons lemon juice
½ teaspoon ginger
¼ teaspoon turmeric
½ teaspoon nutmeg
½ teaspoon coriander
½ teaspoon paprika
⅛ teaspoon cayenne
  pepper
½ teaspoon cinnamon
2 whole boneless chicken
  breasts, split and skinned
½ cup sour cream

In large mixing bowl, combine garlic, lemon juice, ginger, turmeric, nutmeg, coriander, paprika, cayenne pepper and cinnamon. Place chicken breasts in 8-inch baking dish. Pour marinade over chicken. Cover and marinate in refrigerator several hours or overnight. Remove dish from refrigerator; vent plastic wrap. Microwave at HIGH (10) 15 to 20 minutes; turn over after 7 minutes. Top with sour cream.

Total Microwave Cooking Time 15 to 20 Minutes
Makes 4 servings

Chicken Stroganoff

3 tablespoons butter,
  melted, divided
¼ teaspoon salt
¼ teaspoon pepper
6 boneless chicken breast
  halves, skinned and cut
  into 1-inch strips
1 medium onion, sliced
1 cup fresh mushrooms,
  sliced
2 medium zucchini, sliced
1 tablespoon all-purpose
  flour
1 cup chicken broth
½ teaspoon basil
1 (8 oz.) carton sour cream
2 teaspoons dry mustard

In 2-quart casserole, place 2 tablespoons butter, salt and pepper. Toss chicken pieces in butter. Microwave at HIGH (10) 8 to 9 minutes; stir after 4 minutes. Add onion, mushrooms and zucchini to chicken. Microwave at HIGH (10) 4 to 6 minutes; stir after 2 minutes.

In 4-cup glass measure, combine 1 tablespoon melted butter and flour. Add chicken broth and basil; stir well. Microwave at HIGH (10) 4 to 5 minutes, stirring every minute. Add sour cream and mustard; stir to blend. Pour over chicken and vegetables. Microwave at HIGH (10) 3 to 5 minutes until heated through. Serve over rice or egg noodles.

Total Microwave Cooking Time 19 to 25 Minutes
Makes 4 to 6 servings

Fish & Seafood

Baked Lobster Tails

4 (about 8 oz. ea.)
   lobster tails, thawed
3 tablespoons butter,
   melted
⅓ cup seasoned dry
   bread crumbs
⅛ teaspoon onion powder
⅛ teaspoon paprika
⅛ teaspoon salt

With kitchen shears, cut lobster through center of soft shell (underneath) to the tail. Lift lobster out of shell by loosening with fingers, leaving meat attached to tail section. (Lobster meat will rest on shell.) Arrange in 10-inch glass pie plate, tails toward center. In small mixing bowl, combine butter, bread crumbs, onion powder, paprika and salt; sprinkle over lobster. Cover with wax paper. Microwave at MEDIUM HIGH (7) 11 to 13 minutes until lobster is done. Let stand 5 minutes. Serve with Lemon Butter, if desired.

Lemon Butter: In small bowl, Microwave ½ cup butter and 1 to 2 tablespoons lemon juice at MEDIUM (5) 1 to 2 minutes until butter is melted.

Total Microwave Cooking Time 11 to 13 Minutes
Makes 4 servings

Scalloped Oysters

2 tablespoons butter
½ cup onion, chopped
½ cup green pepper,
   chopped
¼ cup butter, melted
2 cups buttery cracker
   crumbs
½ teaspoon salt
⅛ teaspoon pepper
2 (8 oz.) cans fresh oysters,
   drained
1 teaspoon
   Worcestershire sauce
1 cup evaporated milk

In 1-quart casserole, place butter, onion and green pepper. Microwave at HIGH (10) 2 to 3 minutes until tender. Set aside. In small mixing bowl, combine butter, cracker crumbs, salt and pepper. Mix well.

In 2-quart casserole, place ⅓ crumb mixture, one can of oysters and half of onion and green pepper mixture. Repeat layers ending with cracker crumbs.

In small mixing bowl, combine Worcestershire sauce and evaporated milk; pour over layered casserole. Place metal accessory rack on floor of oven. Preheat oven to 350°F. Convection Bake 25 to 35 minutes.

Total Convection Cooking Time 25 to 35 Minutes
Makes 6 servings

Salmon Loaf

2 (16 oz.) cans red salmon,
   drained with bone and
   skin removed
¾ cup dry bread crumbs
½ cup milk
1 egg, beaten
¼ cup butter, melted
½ teaspoon salt
2 tablespoons grated
   Parmesan cheese

In large mixing bowl, combine salmon, bread crumbs, milk, egg, butter, salt and Parmesan cheese. Mix well. Pack mixture firmly into 8x4x3-inch glass loaf dish. Microwave at MEDIUM HIGH (7) 14 to 18 minutes.

TO COOK BY COMBINATION: Place metal accessory rack on floor of oven. Preheat oven to 350°F. Cook on Combination 30 to 35 minutes.

Total Microwave Cooking Time 14 to 18 Minutes
Total Combination Cooking Time 30 to 35 Minutes
Makes 4 to 6 servings

Fish & Seafood

▲ *Salmon Steaks*

Salmon Steaks

Sprinkle lemon pepper onto buttered dish for extra flavor.

1 tablespoon butter
2 teaspoons lemon pepper
6 (5 oz.) salmon steaks
2 teaspoons lemon juice
1 teaspoon lemon pepper
½ teaspoon garlic powder
½ teaspoon onion powder
6 thin onion slices
3 lemon slices, halved
1 teaspoon dried tarragon
1 teaspoon paprika
Dash salt

Place butter in 3-quart oblong glass baking dish. Microwave at HIGH (10) 30 seconds until melted. Coat bottom of dish with butter and sprinkle with lemon pepper. Place salmon steaks in prepared dish. Sprinkle with lemon juice, lemon pepper, garlic powder and onion powder. Place one onion slice and one lemon slice on each salmon steak. Sprinkle with tarragon, paprika and salt. Place metal accessory rack on floor of oven. Preheat oven to 350°F. Cook on Combination 17 to 22 minutes.

Total Combination Cooking Time 17 to 22 Minutes
Makes 6 servings

Shrimp with Dill Sauce

2 tablespoons onion, chopped
1 tablespoon butter
1½ lbs. medium shrimp, uncooked, peeled and deveined
½ cup white wine
3 tablespoons butter, melted
3 tablespoons all-purpose flour
1 cup milk
3 tablespoons lemon juice
¼ teaspoon garlic powder
1 teaspoon dillweed
¼ teaspoon salt

In 2-quart casserole, place onion and butter. Microwave at HIGH (10) 1 to 2 minutes until onion is tender. Add shrimp and wine. Microwave at HIGH (10) 6 to 7 minutes, stirring every 2 minutes.

In medium bowl, combine melted butter and flour, stirring until smooth. Gradually add milk, stirring constantly. Microwave at MEDIUM HIGH (7) 5 to 6 minutes, stirring every 2 minutes. Add lemon juice, garlic powder, dillweed and salt. Pour over shrimp mixture. Mix well. Microwave at HIGH (10) 8 to 10 minutes, stirring every 3 minutes. Serve over rice.

Total Microwave Cooking Time 20 to 25 Minutes
Makes 4 to 6 servings

Fish Almondine

½ cup slivered almonds
¼ cup butter
1 lb. thin fish fillets
1 teaspoon lemon juice
¼ teaspoon salt
⅛ teaspoon pepper
¼ teaspoon dillweed
1 teaspoon fresh parsley, snipped

In 8-inch square baking dish, place almonds and butter. Microwave at HIGH (10) 5 to 6 minutes until almonds are golden brown. Remove almonds and set aside. Place fish in baking dish, turning to coat both sides with butter. Sprinkle with lemon juice, salt, pepper, dillweed, parsley and almonds. Cover with wax paper. Microwave at HIGH (10) 4 to 6 minutes until fish flakes easily when tested with a fork. Let stand 1 minute before serving.

TO COOK BY COMBINATION: Place metal accessory rack on floor of oven. Preheat oven to 350°F. Cook on Combination 7 to 10 minutes.

TO COOK BY CONVECTION: Place metal accessory rack on floor of oven. Preheat oven to 350°F. Convection Bake 12 to 15 minutes.

Total Microwave Cooking Time 9 to 12 Minutes
Total Combination Cooking Time 7 to 10 Minutes
Total Convection Cooking Time 12 to 15 Minutes
Makes 2 servings

Shrimp Enchiladas

¼ cup butter, melted
½ cup sweet red pepper, chopped
½ cup onion, minced
½ cup green pepper, chopped
¼ teaspoon garlic powder
½ teaspoon oregano
½ teaspoon salt
⅛ teaspoon pepper
⅛ teaspoon cayenne pepper
¾ cup whipping cream
1 tablespoon all-purpose flour
3 cups Monterey Jack cheese, divided
½ cup sour cream
¼ cup butter, melted
1 lb. medium shrimp, uncooked, peeled and deveined
1 cup onion, chopped and divided
2 cups tomatoes, peeled and chopped, divided
8 (9-inch) flour tortillas

In 2-quart casserole, place butter, red pepper, onion and green pepper. Microwave at HIGH (10) 4 to 5 minutes; stir after 2 minutes. Add garlic powder, oregano, salt, pepper, cayenne pepper, cream and flour. Blend well. Microwave at HIGH (10) 3 to 5 minutes; stir after 2 minutes. Add 1½ cups cheese; stir until melted. Add sour cream; stir to blend.

In medium bowl, place butter, shrimp and ½ cup onion. Microwave at HIGH (10) 4 to 5 minutes; stir after 2 minutes. Chop shrimp and return to butter and onion. Add 1 cup tomatoes and ½ of cream sauce. Spoon ⅓ cup shrimp mixture into each tortilla. Roll up tightly. Arrange, seam side down, in 3-quart oblong glass baking dish. Spoon remaining cream sauce over tortillas. Place metal accessory rack on floor of oven. Preheat oven to 350°F. Convection Bake 30 to 40 minutes. Sprinkle enchiladas with remaining 1½ cups cheese, ½ cup onion and 1 cup tomatoes.

Total Convection Cooking Time 30 to 40 Minutes
Makes 4 servings

Fish & Seafood

▲ *Creamy Crabmeat and Almonds*

Creamy Crabmeat and Almonds

½ cup fresh mushrooms, sliced
1 small green pepper, cut in thin strips
2 tablespoons butter
2 (6 oz.) cans crabmeat, drained and flaked
⅓ cup slivered almonds
1 tablespoon orange juice
1 teaspoon lemon juice
2 (10 ½ oz.) cans cream of celery soup
⅓ cup ripe olives, quartered
¼ cup pimento, chopped and drained
2 tablespoons fresh parsley, snipped
¼ teaspoon hot sauce
¼ teaspoon pepper

In 3-quart casserole, combine mushrooms, green pepper and butter. Microwave at HIGH (10) 2 to 3 minutes until mushrooms are tender. Add crabmeat, almonds, orange juice, lemon juice, celery soup, olives, pimento, parsley, hot sauce and pepper. Cover with wax paper. Microwave at HIGH (10) 10 to 12 minutes; stir after 6 minutes. Let stand covered 5 minutes. Serve over rice.

Total Microwave Cooking Time 12 to 15 Minutes
Makes 6 to 8 servings

Tuna Croquettes with Lemon Sauce

1 cup dry bread crumbs
1 (6 ½ oz.) can water-
  packed tuna, drained
1 cup carrots, grated
½ cup milk
½ cup celery, diced
1 egg, beaten
1 tablespoon onion,
  minced
½ teaspoon salt
¼ teaspoon pepper

Lemon Sauce:
1 cup milk, divided
1 tablespoon cornstarch
2 tablespoons butter,
  melted
⅛ teaspoon pepper
⅓ cup fresh parsley,
  snipped
1 ½ tablespoons lemon
  juice

Place metal accessory rack on floor of oven. Preheat oven to 375°F.

In large mixing bowl, combine dry bread crumbs, tuna, carrots, milk, celery, egg, onion, salt and pepper. Mix well. Shape into 6 cone-shaped portions. Place on greased baking sheet. Convection Bake 18 to 20 minutes. Serve with lemon sauce.

Total Convection Cooking Time 18 to 20 Minutes
Makes 4 to 6 servings

In small mixing bowl, combine ¼ cup milk and corn-starch; stir until smooth. Add remaining ¾ cup milk, butter and pepper. Microwave at HIGH (10) 3 to 4 minutes; stir after 2 minutes. Add parsley and lemon juice.

Total Microwave Cooking Time 3 to 4 Minutes
Makes 1 cup

Shape tuna mixture into 6 cone shaped portions.

Shrimp Pilaf

¼ cup butter
½ cup onion,
  thinly sliced
⅓ cup green pepper, diced
2 cups instant rice
2 cups hot water
2 (8 oz.) cans tomato sauce
1 teaspoon seasoned salt
¼ teaspoon pepper
¼ teaspoon prepared
  mustard
1 ½ cups canned shrimp

In 2-quart casserole, place butter, onion and green pepper. Microwave at HIGH (10) 4 to 5 minutes; stir after 2 minutes. Add rice, water, tomato sauce, seasoned salt, pepper, mustard and shrimp. Mix well. Microwave at HIGH (10) 9 to 11 minutes, stirring every 3 minutes.

Total Microwave Cooking Time 13 to 16 Minutes
Makes 6 servings

Scallops In Wine Sauce

½ cup hot water
¾ lb. scallops
3 tablespoons butter
½ teaspoon garlic powder
2 green onions, chopped
¼ teaspoon paprika
2 tablespoons dry white
  wine
1 tablespoon lemon juice

In 2-quart casserole, place water and scallops. Cover. Microwave at HIGH (10) 3 to 5 minutes, until scallops are opaque; stir after 2 minutes. Drain and set aside.

In 2-cup glass measure, combine butter, garlic powder, onions, paprika, wine and lemon juice. Microwave at HIGH (10) 2 to 4 minutes. Pour over scallops.

Total Microwave Cooking Time 5 to 9 Minutes
Makes 2 to 3 servings

Fish & Seafood

▲ *Scallops Oriental*

Scallops Oriental

1 lb. fresh scallops
½ cup water
1½ cups carrots,
  thinly sliced
2 tablespoons green onion,
  sliced
¼ teaspoon garlic powder
1 tablespoon vegetable oil
1 tablespoon cornstarch
¾ teaspoon sugar
½ teaspoon ground ginger
½ cup chicken broth
2 tablespoons soy sauce
2 tablespoons dry sherry
1 (6 oz.) pkg. frozen
  snow peas, thawed

In 2-quart casserole, place scallops and water. Cover. Microwave at HIGH (10) 4 to 6 minutes, until scallops are opaque, stirring every 2 minutes. Drain and set aside.

In 2-quart casserole, combine carrots, green onion, garlic powder and oil. Cover. Microwave at HIGH (10) 3 to 4 minutes until vegetables are crisp-tender. Stir in cornstarch, sugar, ginger, chicken broth, soy sauce and sherry. Microwave at HIGH (10) 2 to 3 minutes, until thickened, stirring every minute. Add snow peas. Microwave at HIGH (10) 2 to 3 minutes, until snow peas are crisp-tender, stirring every minute. Add scallops. Microwave at HIGH (10) 1 to 2 minutes until heated through.

Total Microwave Cooking Time 12 to 18 Minutes
Makes 4 to 6 servings

Baked Fish with Cheese

1 lb. haddock
½ teaspoon seasoned salt
1 tablespoon tarragon
2 tablespoons butter
¼ cup sour cream or
  yogurt
1 cup mozzarella cheese,
  shredded

Arrange fish in 2-quart oblong glass baking dish. Sprinkle with seasoned salt and tarragon. Dot with butter; cover with wax paper. Microwave at HIGH (10) 2 to 3 minutes. Set aside. In small mixing bowl, blend sour cream or yogurt and mozzarella cheese. Spread mixture on fish and cover with wax paper. Microwave at HIGH (10) 2 to 3 minutes.

TO COOK BY CONVECTION: Place metal accessory rack on floor of oven. Preheat oven to 350°F. Convection Bake fish 10 to 15 minutes. Top with cheese mixture and continue to bake 5 to 10 minutes longer.

Total Microwave Cooking Time 4 to 6 Minutes
Total Convection Cooking Time 15 to 25 Minutes
Makes 3 to 4 servings

Baked Scrod

2 tablespoons olive oil
1 cup onion, thinly sliced
½ teaspoon garlic powder
2 cups fresh mushrooms,
    thinly sliced
1 bay leaf
1 teaspoon thyme
2 teaspoons oregano
⅛ teaspoon salt
¼ teaspoon lemon pepper
2 tablespoons oil
2 lbs. scrod, cut into
    4 equal portions
2 teaspoons fresh parsley,
    snipped

In 2-quart casserole, combine olive oil, onion, garlic powder, mushrooms, bay leaf, thyme, oregano, salt and lemon pepper. Microwave at HIGH (10) 4 to 5 minutes until onion is transparent and mushrooms are tender.

Place metal accessory rack on floor of oven. Preheat oven to 450°F. Cut aluminum foil into 4 (18 x 12-inch) pieces. Brush aluminum foil with oil and place fish portions on the foil. Spoon ¼ of filling over each portion of fish. Sprinkle with parsley. Fold foil, crimping edges to seal. Place foil wrapped fish on baking sheet. Convection Bake 15 to 20 minutes.

Total Convection Cooking Time 15 to 20 Minutes
Makes 4 servings

Place fish on foil and spoon ¼ of vegetable filling over each portion.

Seafood Marinara

2 tablespoons butter,
    melted
¼ teaspoon garlic powder
2 tomatoes, peeled and
    chopped
1 tablespoon tomato paste
¼ cup white wine
¾ teaspoon basil
¼ teaspoon lemon pepper
2 teaspoons fresh parsley,
    snipped
½ lb. scallops
½ lb. shrimp, uncooked,
    peeled and deveined

In 1-quart casserole, combine butter, garlic powder, tomatoes, tomato paste, wine, basil, lemon pepper and parsley. Microwave at HIGH (10) 5 to 6 minutes; stir after 3 minutes. Puree tomato mixture in blender at high speed for 1 minute.

In 2-quart casserole, place scallops and shrimp. Add tomato mixture. Microwave at HIGH (10) 5 to 7 minutes. Let stand 5 minutes. Serve over pasta.

Total Microwave Cooking Time 10 to 13 Minutes
Makes 4 servings

Completely enclose fish in foil, and crimp edges to seal.

Italian Haddock

2 tablespoons olive oil
1 tablespoon lemon juice
1 cup tomatoes, chopped
1½ cups fresh mushrooms,
    sliced
¼ cup onion, chopped
¼ cup green pepper,
    chopped
2 tablespoons fresh
    parsley, snipped
¼ teaspoon garlic powder
¾ teaspoon oregano
½ teaspoon seasoned salt
1 (16 oz.) pkg. frozen
    haddock fillets, thawed

In 2-quart casserole, combine olive oil, lemon juice, tomatoes, mushrooms, onion, green pepper, parsley, garlic powder, oregano and seasoned salt. Cover. Microwave at HIGH (10) 4 to 6 minutes, until onion is tender; stir after 2 minutes.

Place fish fillets in 2-quart oblong glass baking dish. Spoon vegetable mixture over fillets. Cover with vented plastic wrap. Microwave at HIGH (10) 2 to 4 minutes until fish flakes easily. Rotate dish ½ turn after 1½ minutes. Let stand 2 to 3 minutes.

Total Microwave Cooking Time 6 to 10 Minutes
Makes 4 to 6 servings

Chicken Pot Pie

2 whole chicken breasts,
   split and skinned
2 ½ cups water
Leaves from 2 stalks celery
½ teaspoon salt
3 tablespoons vegetable oil
½ cup green onion,
   chopped
½ cup celery, chopped
⅓ cup all-purpose flour
1 (2 oz.) jar sliced pimento
1 (10 oz.) pkg. frozen peas
   and carrots, thawed
½ teaspoon pepper
1 teaspoon thyme
Pastry for 2 (9-inch)
   pie crusts

In 3-quart casserole, place chicken, water, celery leaves and salt. Microwave at HIGH (10) 14 to 17 minutes. Remove chicken breasts and celery leaves, reserving broth. Cut chicken breasts into ½-inch cubes.

In 3-quart oblong glass baking dish, place oil, green onion and celery. Microwave at HIGH (10) 2 to 3 minutes until vegetables are crisp-tender. Stir in flour until smooth. Add chicken broth. Microwave at HIGH (10) 5 to 6 minutes, until thickened, stirring every 2 minutes. Add chicken, pimento, peas and carrots, pepper and thyme. Top with pie crust, crimping edges of crust around inside of dish. Decorate with pastry cut-outs if desired. Vent crust to allow steam to escape. Place metal accessory rack on floor of oven. Preheat oven to 400°F. Bake on Combination 20 to 25 minutes.

Total Combination Cooking Time 20 to 25 Minutes
Makes 8 servings

Lasagna

1 lb. ground beef
½ cup onion, chopped
2 (8 oz.) cans tomato sauce
1 (6 oz.) can tomato paste
1 ½ teaspoons oregano
1 ¾ teaspoons basil
¾ teaspoon garlic salt
1 teaspoon parsley flakes
1 (12 oz.) carton small curd
   cottage cheese
1 egg, beaten
¼ teaspoon seasoned salt
6 lasagna noodles, cooked
1 (12 oz.) pkg. shredded
   mozzarella cheese
½ cup grated Parmesan
   cheese

In 2-quart casserole, place beef and onion. Cover. Microwave at HIGH (10) 5 to 7 minutes, until beef is thoroughly cooked; stir after 3 minutes. Drain. Add tomato sauce, tomato paste, oregano, basil, garlic salt and parsley flakes. Set aside.

In small mixing bowl, combine cottage cheese, egg and seasoned salt.

In 2-quart oblong glass baking dish, spread ⅓ of meat sauce over bottom. Top with half of lasagna noodles, half of cottage cheese mixture and half of mozzarella cheese. Repeat layers, ending with meat sauce. Place metal accessory rack on floor of oven. Preheat oven to 375°F. Cook on Combination 25 minutes. Sprinkle with Parmesan cheese and continue cooking on Combination 8 to 10 minutes.

TO COOK BY CONVECTION: Place metal accessory rack on floor of oven. Preheat oven to 350°F. Bake 35 to 45 minutes.

Total Combination Cooking Time 33 to 35 Minutes
Total Convection Cooking Time 35 to 45 Minutes
Makes 4 to 6 servings

Casseroles

▲ *Vegetable Lasagna*

Wear gloves when chopping hot peppers to protect from burning reaction.

Noodles Con Carne

½ **lb. ground beef**
½ **lb. hot bulk sausage**
¼ **cup onion, chopped**
½ **cup green pepper, chopped**
½ **teaspoon salt**
⅛ **teaspoon pepper**
1 **hot pepper, chopped (optional)**
1 **(15 oz.) can chili beans**
1½ **tablespoons chili powder**
1 **(8 oz.) can tomato sauce**
2 **cups Cheddar cheese, shredded**
6 **oz. wide egg noodles, cooked and drained**

In 3-quart casserole, crumble ground beef, sausage, onion, green pepper, salt, pepper and hot pepper. Microwave at HIGH (10) 8 to 10 minutes, until meat is browned and onion is tender, stirring every 3 minutes. Drain. Add chili beans, chili powder, tomato sauce, Cheddar cheese and egg noodles, mixing well. Microwave at HIGH (10) 12 to 15 minutes until bubbly.

TO COOK BY COMBINATION: Place metal accessory rack on floor of oven. Preheat oven to 350°F. Bake on Combination 28 to 33 minutes until bubbly.

Total Microwave Cooking Time 20 to 25 Minutes
Total Combination Cooking Time 28 to 33 Minutes
Makes 12 servings

Vegetable Lasagna

1 large onion, chopped
½ lb. carrots, shredded
½ lb. fresh mushrooms, coarsely chopped
2 cups small curd cottage cheese
2 eggs
¼ cup grated Parmesan cheese
1 teaspoon oregano
1 (14 oz.) jar spaghetti sauce, divided
6 lasagna noodles, cooked
1 (10 oz.) pkg. frozen chopped spinach, thawed and drained
½ lb. tomatoes, peeled and coarsely chopped
2 cups mozzarella cheese, shredded

In 2-quart casserole, combine onion, carrots and mushrooms; cover. Microwave at HIGH (10) 5 to 8 minutes until vegetables are tender. Drain and set aside. In small mixing bowl, combine cottage cheese, eggs, Parmesan cheese and oregano.

In 2-quart oblong glass baking dish, layer half of spaghetti sauce, 3 lasagna noodles, all onion-carrot-mushroom mixture and half of cheese mixture.

Cover with remaining noodles, spaghetti sauce, spinach and cheese mixture. Top with tomatoes and mozzarella cheese. Microwave at HIGH (10) 19 to 22 minutes.

TO COOK BY COMBINATION: Place metal accessory rack on floor of oven. Preheat oven to 350°F. Cook on Combination 30 to 35 minutes.

TO COOK BY CONVECTION: Place metal accessory rack on floor of oven. Preheat oven to 350°F. Convection Bake 40 to 45 minutes.

Total Microwave Cooking Time 24 to 30 Minutes
Total Combination Cooking Time 30 to 35 Minutes
Total Convection Cooking Time 40 to 45 Minutes
Makes 6 servings

Spread half of cheese mixture over mixed vegetables to form first layer.

Form the second layer with remaining ingredients, starting with the noodles.

Italian Beef and Rice Casserole

1 lb. ground beef
1 cup onion, chopped
½ cup green pepper, chopped
½ cup celery, chopped
1 (14 ½ oz.) can tomatoes
1 (6 oz.) can Italian tomato paste
1 (4 oz.) can mushroom pieces, drained
2 tablespoons fresh parsley, snipped
½ teaspoon salt
¼ teaspoon thyme
½ teaspoon pepper
¼ teaspoon marjoram
1 cup rice, cooked
1 cup Cheddar cheese, shredded

In 2-quart casserole, combine ground beef, onion, green pepper and celery. Microwave at HIGH (10) 5 to 7 minutes until vegetables are tender. Drain. Add tomatoes, tomato paste, mushrooms, parsley, salt, thyme, pepper, marjoram and rice. Microwave at HIGH (10) 15 to 18 minutes. Top with Cheddar cheese and continue to Microwave at HIGH (10) 2 to 3 minutes.

TO COOK BY COMBINATION: Place metal accessory rack on floor of oven. Preheat oven to 350°F. Cook on Combination 25 to 30 minutes. Top with Cheddar cheese and continue to cook 5 minutes.

TO COOK BY CONVECTION: Place metal accessory rack on floor of oven. Preheat oven to 350°F. Convection Bake 35 to 40 minutes. Top with Cheddar cheese and continue to cook 5 minutes.

Total Microwave Cooking Time 22 to 28 Minutes
Total Combination Cooking Time 30 to 35 Minutes
Total Convection Cooking Time 40 to 45 Minutes
Makes 6 servings

Casseroles

Yellow Squash Casserole

**6 cups yellow squash,
  coarsely chopped**
½ cup water
**1 dozen round buttery
  crackers, crushed**
**1 (3 oz.) pkg. cream
  cheese, softened**
**1 (10 ¾ oz.) can cream of
  chicken soup**
1 egg
¼ cup butter, melted
3 small carrots, grated
**½ cup onion,
  finely chopped**
**½ cup herb-seasoned
  stuffing mix**

In 2-quart casserole, combine squash and water. Cover. Microwave at HIGH (10) 10 minutes; stir after 5 minutes. Drain well.

Place metal accessory rack on floor of oven. Preheat oven to 350°F. Place crackers in greased 2-quart oblong glass baking dish. In medium mixing bowl, combine cream cheese, soup, egg and butter. Stir until smooth. Stir in squash, carrots and onion. Spoon into prepared baking dish; sprinkle with stuffing mix. Convection Bake 30 to 40 minutes.

TO COOK BY COMBINATION: Place metal accessory rack on floor of oven. Preheat oven to 350°F. Cook on Combination 25 to 30 minutes.

Total Convection Cooking Time 30 to 40 Minutes
Total Combination Cooking Time 25 to 30 Minutes
Makes 10 to 12 servings

Creamed Spaghetti with Turkey Casserole

**1 ¼ cups spaghetti, broken
  into 2-inch pieces,
  cooked and drained**
**1 ½ cups cooked turkey,
  cubed**
⅓ cup onion, chopped
⅓ cup water
**¼ cup green pepper,
  chopped**
1 (2 oz.) jar sliced pimento
**1 (10 ¾ oz.) can cream of
  mushroom soup**
¼ teaspoon salt
¼ teaspoon pepper
**2 cups Cheddar cheese,
  shredded**

In 2-quart oblong glass baking dish, combine cooked spaghetti, turkey, onion, water, green pepper, pimento, soup, salt, pepper and cheese. Mix well. Microwave at MEDIUM HIGH (7) 18 to 21 minutes.

TO COOK BY COMBINATION: Place metal accessory rack on floor of oven. Preheat oven to 350°F. Bake on Combination 25 to 30 minutes.

Total Microwave Cooking Time 18 to 21 Minutes
Total Combination Cooking Time 25 to 30 Minutes
Makes 6 servings

Layered Supper

2 medium potatoes, sliced
2 medium carrots, sliced
**⅓ cup long grain rice,
  uncooked**
2 small onions, sliced
**1 lb. ground beef, cooked
  and drained**
1 (28 oz.) can tomatoes
2 tablespoons brown sugar

In 2-quart casserole, layer potatoes, carrots, rice, onions, ground beef and tomatoes. Sprinkle brown sugar on top. Microwave at HIGH (10) 25 to 30 minutes.

TO COOK BY COMBINATION: Place metal accessory rack on floor of oven. Preheat oven to 350°F. Cook on Combination 45 to 50 minutes.

Total Microwave Cooking Time 25 to 30 Minutes
Total Combination Cooking Time 45 to 50 Minutes
Makes 4 servings

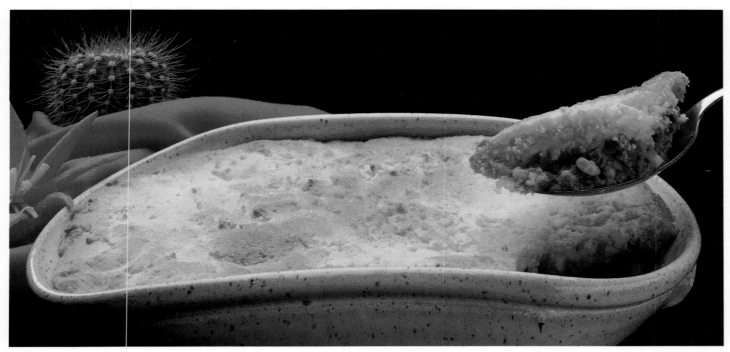

▲ *Tamale Pie*

Tamale Pie

1 (8 ½ oz.) pkg. corn
  muffin mix
1 egg
⅓ cup milk
1 lb. ground beef
¼ lb. bulk pork sausage
¼ cup onion, chopped
⅛ teaspoon garlic powder
1 (14 ½ oz.) can stewed
  tomatoes, drained
1 (15 ¼ oz.) can whole
  kernel corn, drained
1 (6 oz.) can tomato paste
2 teaspoons chili powder
½ teaspoon salt
⅓ cup pitted ripe olives,
  sliced
½ cup Cheddar cheese,
  shredded
Dash paprika

In small mixing bowl, combine corn muffin mix, egg and milk just until moistened.

In 8-inch square baking dish, combine ground beef, sausage, onion and garlic. Microwave at HIGH (10) 6 to 9 minutes, until meat loses pink color; stir every 3 minutes. Drain. Stir in tomatoes, corn, tomato paste, chili powder, salt and olives. Spread corn muffin mixture over meat mixture.

Place metal accessory rack on floor of oven. Preheat oven to 350°F. Convection Bake 26 to 31 minutes until center is set. Sprinkle with cheese and paprika, continue to bake for 4 minutes until cheese melts.

TO COOK BY COMBINATION: Place metal accessory rack on floor of oven. Preheat oven to 400°F. Cook on Combination 22 to 26 minutes. Sprinkle with cheese and paprika; continue to cook 3 to 4 minutes until cheese melts.

Total Convection Cooking Time 30 to 35 Minutes
Total Combination Cooking Time 25 to 30 Minutes
Makes 4 to 6 servings

Evenly spread corn muffin mixture over beef mixture and bake.

Casseroles

▲ *Simple Tuna Casserole*

Toss bread cubes in melted butter until coated evenly.

Simple Tuna Casserole

3 tablespoons butter
2 tablespoons onion, chopped
3 tablespoons all-purpose flour
½ teaspoon salt
¼ teaspoon pepper
1½ cups milk
2 (6½ oz.) cans tuna, drained
2 cups soft bread cubes
2 tablespoons butter, melted
1 (10 oz.) pkg. frozen peas, cooked
1 medium carrot, shredded
1 cup sharp Cheddar cheese, shredded

In 2-quart casserole, place butter and onion. Microwave at HIGH (10) 2 to 3 minutes until onion is transparent. Add flour, salt, pepper and milk. Stir well to blend. Microwave at HIGH (10) 5 to 6 minutes, until thickened, stirring every 2 minutes. Add tuna.

In 8-inch square glass baking dish, toss bread cubes in melted butter. Add peas and carrot. Pour cream sauce over vegetables and top with cheese.

Place metal accessory rack on floor of oven. Preheat oven to 350°F. Cook on Combination 18 to 23 minutes.

TO COOK BY CONVECTION: Place metal accessory rack on floor of oven. Preheat oven to 350°F. Convection Bake 25 to 30 minutes.

Total Combination Cooking Time 18 to 23 Minutes
Total Convection Cooking Time 25 to 30 Minutes
Makes 4 servings

Hamburger & Zucchini Casserole

1½ lbs. ground chuck
1 medium onion, chopped
1 (14½ oz.) can tomatoes, undrained
1 (15 oz.) can tomato sauce
½ teaspoon garlic powder
½ teaspoon salt
¼ teaspoon pepper
1 (15¼ oz.) can whole kernel corn, drained
3 small zucchini, diced

In 3-quart casserole, combine beef and onion. Microwave at HIGH (10) 5 to 7 minutes; stir after 3 minutes. Drain. Add tomatoes, tomato sauce, garlic powder, salt, pepper, corn and zucchini. Stir well. Cover. Microwave at HIGH (10) 19 to 23 minutes; stir after 9 minutes. Let stand, covered, 5 minutes before serving.

Total Microwave Cooking Time 24 to 30 Minutes
Makes 6 to 8 servings

Hearty Bean Casserole

1 ½ lbs. ground beef
½ cup catsup
½ teaspoon dry mustard
2 tablespoons vinegar
¼ cup dark molasses
⅓ cup onion, minced
1 (17 oz.) can lima beans,
    drained
1 (15 ½ oz.) can red kidney
    beans, drained
1 (16 oz.) can pork and
    beans
1 (8 oz.) can tomato sauce
½ teaspoon salt
½ teaspoon hot sauce

In 3-quart casserole, place ground beef. Microwave at HIGH (10) 6 to 7 minutes, until beef is thoroughly cooked, stirring every 2 minutes. Drain. Add catsup, dry mustard, vinegar, molasses, onion, lima beans, kidney beans, pork and beans, tomato sauce, salt and hot sauce; cover. Microwave at MEDIUM HIGH (7) 15 to 18 minutes; stir after 8 minutes.

TO COOK BY COMBINATION: Place metal accessory rack on floor of oven. Preheat oven to 375°F. Cook on Combination 20 to 25 minutes.

TO COOK BY CONVECTION: Place metal accessory rack on floor of oven. Preheat oven to 350°F. Convection Bake 30 to 40 minutes.

Total Microwave Cooking Time 21 to 25 Minutes
Total Combination Cooking Time 20 to 25 Minutes
Total Convection Cooking Time 30 to 40 Minutes
Makes 8 servings

Spicy Wild Rice Casserole

1 lb. hot bulk sausage
½ cup celery, chopped
½ cup onion, chopped
½ cup mushrooms, sliced
½ cup green pepper,
    chopped
1 ½ cups water
1 (10 ¾ oz.) can cream of
    mushroom soup
1 (6 oz.) pkg. long grain
    and wild rice
1 cup Cheddar cheese,
    shredded
¼ teaspoon pepper

In 2-quart casserole, combine sausage, celery, onion, mushrooms and green pepper. Microwave at HIGH (10) 8 to 10 minutes, stirring every 3 minutes. Drain. Add water, soup, rice, cheese and pepper; cover. Place metal accessory rack on floor of oven. Preheat oven to 350°F. Convection Bake 1 hour. Let stand 5 minutes before serving.

TO COOK BY COMBINATION: Place metal accessory rack on floor of oven. Preheat oven to 350°F. Cook on Combination 35 to 40 minutes. Let stand 5 minutes before serving.

Total Convection Cooking Time 1 Hour
Total Combination Cooking Time 35 to 40 Minutes
Makes 6 to 8 servings

Spinach with Artichokes Casserole

1 (8 oz.) pkg. cream cheese
2 tablespoons mayonnaise
4 tablespoons butter
6 tablespoons milk
1 (14 oz.) can artichoke
    hearts, drained
2 (10 oz.) pkgs. frozen
    chopped spinach,
    thawed and drained
Dash pepper
⅓ cup grated Parmesan
    cheese

Place metal accessory rack on floor of oven. Preheat oven to 350°F. In medium mixing bowl, combine cream cheese, mayonnaise and butter. Beat with an electric mixer for 2 minutes until light and fluffy. Gradually beat in milk.

In 3-quart casserole, place artichokes and layer spinach on top of artichokes. Spread cream cheese mixture over top of spinach. Sprinkle with pepper and Parmesan cheese. Convection Bake 25 to 30 minutes until top is lightly browned.

Total Convection Cooking Time 25 to 30 Minutes
Makes 10 to 12 servings

Drain spinach thoroughly before adding to the artichokes.

Casseroles

▲ *Chicken Enchiladas*

Chicken Enchiladas

**4 (5 oz.) cans cooked
    chicken**
1 cup sour cream
**1 (10 ¾ oz.) can cream of
    chicken soup**
**1 ½ cups Monterey Jack
    cheese, shredded**
**1 ½ cups Colby cheese,
    shredded**
**1 (4 oz.) can chopped
    green chilies, drained**
**2 tablespoons onion,
    chopped**
¼ teaspoon pepper
10 (10-inch) flour tortillas
**1 cup Colby cheese,
    shredded**

Place metal accessory rack on floor of oven. Preheat oven to 350°F. In large mixing bowl, combine chicken, sour cream, soup, cheeses, green chilies, onion and pepper. Mix well. Place ½ cup of mixture on each tortilla; roll up and place seam side down in 3-quart oblong glass baking dish. Convection Bake 25 to 35 minutes. Sprinkle with 1 cup Colby cheese and continue to bake 5 minutes longer.

TO COOK BY COMBINATION: Place metal accessory rack on floor of oven. Preheat oven to 350°F. Cook on Combination 20 to 25 minutes. Sprinkle with 1 cup Colby cheese and continue to cook 5 minutes longer.

Total Convection Cooking Time 35 to 40 Minutes
Total Combination Cooking Time 25 to 30 Minutes
Makes 5 servings

Enchilada Casserole

2 lbs. ground beef
1 medium onion, chopped
2 (8 oz.) cans tomato sauce
1 (12 oz.) can Mexicorn, drained
½ cup ripe olives, sliced
1 (10 oz.) can hot enchilada sauce
¼ teaspoon chili powder
¼ teaspoon pepper
½ teaspoon salt
½ teaspoon oregano
12 corn tortillas, divided
2 cups Cheddar cheese, shredded, divided

In 3-quart casserole, combine ground beef and onion. Cover. Microwave at HIGH (10) 8 to 10 minutes, until meat is thoroughly cooked; stir after 5 minutes. Drain. Add tomato sauce, corn, ripe olives, enchilada sauce, chili powder, pepper, salt and oregano. Microwave at HIGH (10) 3 to 5 minutes.

Place 6 tortillas on bottom of 3-quart oblong glass baking dish. Pour half of meat mixture over tortillas. Sprinkle 1 cup of cheese on top. Repeat layers. Microwave at HIGH (10) 12 to 15 minutes.

TO COOK BY COMBINATION: Place metal accessory rack on floor of oven. Preheat oven to 350°F. Cook on Combination 30 to 35 minutes.

TO COOK BY CONVECTION: Place metal accessory rack on floor of oven. Preheat oven to 350°F. Convection Bake 35 to 40 minutes.

Total Microwave Cooking Time 23 to 30 Minutes
Total Combination Cooking Time 30 to 35 Minutes
Total Convection Cooking Time 35 to 40 Minutes
Makes 8 servings

Place 6 tortillas in dish to start first layer.

Sprinkle first layer with cheese and repeat layers.

Cheesy Chicken Casserole

¼ cup butter
¼ cup onion, chopped
⅓ cup green pepper, chopped
½ cup mushrooms, sliced
6 tablespoons all-purpose flour
1 (14 ½ oz.) can chicken broth
1 cup milk
½ teaspoon salt
⅛ teaspoon pepper
1 (8 oz.) pkg. medium egg noodles, cooked
3 (5 oz.) cans cooked chicken
1 cup Cheddar cheese, shredded

In 3-quart casserole, combine butter, onion, green pepper and mushrooms. Cover with vented plastic wrap. Microwave at HIGH (10) 4 to 6 minutes, until tender, stirring every 2 minutes. Add flour, chicken broth, milk, salt and pepper. Stir well. Microwave at HIGH (10) 4 to 6 minutes, stirring with wire whisk every 2 minutes. Add noodles and chicken. Top with Cheddar cheese. Microwave at HIGH (10) 12 to 15 minutes until heated through.

TO COOK BY COMBINATION: Place metal accessory rack on floor of oven. Preheat oven to 350°F. Cook on Combination 20 to 24 minutes.

TO COOK BY CONVECTION: Place metal accessory rack on floor of oven. Preheat oven to 350°F. Convection Bake 25 to 30 minutes.

Total Microwave Cooking Time 20 to 27 Minutes
Total Combination Cooking Time 20 to 24 Minutes
Total Convection Cooking Time 25 to 30 Minutes
Makes 6 servings

Eggs & Cheese

Normandy Omelet

2 tablespoons butter,
    divided, melted
4 eggs, separated
Salt and pepper to taste
1 cup fresh strawberries,
    sliced
1 tablespoon honey
Confectioners sugar,
    optional

In 9-inch pie plate, place 1 tablespoon melted butter. Turn plate to coat bottom. Set aside. In small mixing bowl, beat egg whites until stiff, but not dry. In 4-cup glass measure, beat egg yolks, salt and pepper until thickened. Fold egg yolks into egg whites; carefully pour mixture into pie plate. Microwave at MEDIUM (5) 4 to 5 minutes. Let stand 2 minutes. With spatula, loosen edges of omelet from plate.

In 1-quart casserole, combine strawberries, honey and remaining butter. Mix well. Spoon strawberries onto half of omelet. Fold other half over strawberries. Sprinkle with confectioners sugar, if desired.

TO COOK BY CONVECTION: Place metal accessory rack on floor of oven. Preheat oven to 325°F. Convection Bake 18 to 22 minutes. With spatula, loosen edges of omelet from plate. Spoon strawberries onto half of omelet. Fold other half over strawberries. Sprinkle with confectioners sugar, if desired.

Total Microwave Cooking Time 4 to 5 Minutes
Total Convection Cooking Time 18 to 22 Minutes
Makes 1 serving

Garlic Cheese and Grits Casserole

3 cups hot tap water
¾ cup quick cooking grits
¾ teaspoon salt
5 tablespoons butter,
    sliced
1½ cups sharp Cheddar
    cheese, shredded
2 eggs, beaten
Milk
¼ teaspoon garlic powder
Dash hot sauce
½ cup sharp Cheddar
    cheese, shredded
Paprika

In 3-quart casserole, place water, grits and salt. Microwave at HIGH (10) 10 to 12 minutes; stir after 5 minutes. Add butter and cheese to grits. Stir well until melted. In 1-cup glass measure, beat eggs, add enough milk to total ¾ cup. Add garlic powder and hot sauce. Quickly stir into grits. Pour into well greased 8-inch square baking dish. Sprinkle cheese over top. Sprinkle with paprika. Place metal accessory rack on floor of oven. Preheat oven to 350°F. Cook on Combination 30 to 35 minutes until knife inserted in center comes out clean. Let stand 5 minutes before serving.

TO COOK BY CONVECTION: Place metal accessory rack on floor of oven. Preheat oven to 325°F. Convection Bake 35 to 40 minutes until knife inserted in center comes out clean.

Total Combination Cooking Time 30 to 35 Minutes
Total Convection Cooking Time 35 to 40 Minutes
Makes 6 servings

Eggs & Cheese

▲ *Asparagus Egg Roll-Up With Cheese Sauce*

Basic Omelet

1 ½   teaspoons butter
1 ½   teaspoons peanut oil
3   eggs, at room
    temperature
1   tablespoon water
⅛   teaspoon salt
Dash pepper

In 9-inch pie plate, place butter and peanut oil. Microwave at HIGH (10) 30 to 45 seconds until melted. Turn plate to coat bottom with butter and oil. In medium mixing bowl, combine eggs, water, salt and pepper. Beat with a wire whisk until blended. Pour mixture into pie plate. Cover with vented plastic wrap. Microwave at MEDIUM (5) 2 to 3 minutes, until omelet is almost set; stir after 1 minute. Let stand, covered, 2 minutes. Using a spatula, loosen edges of omelet from plate; fold over and serve.

Total Microwave Cooking Time 2½ to 3¾ Minutes
Makes 1 serving

Mushroom Omelet

1   tablespoon onion,
    chopped
½   cup fresh mushrooms,
    sliced
1   tablespoon butter
⅛   teaspoon salt
⅛   teaspoon pepper
⅛   teaspoon nutmeg

In 1 ½-quart casserole, place onions, mushrooms and butter. Microwave at HIGH (10) 2 to 3 minutes until onions are transparent and mushrooms are tender. Add salt, pepper and nutmeg. Prepare Basic Omelet. Fill prepared omelet with mushroom mixture and fold over to serve.

Total Microwave Cooking Time 2 to 3 Minutes
Makes 1 serving

Garlic & Potato Omelet

1   small new potato, sliced
1   slice bacon, cooked and
    diced
1   tablespoon green onion,
    chopped
⅛   teaspoon garlic powder
⅛   teaspoon salt
Dash pepper

In 1-quart casserole, place potato slices. Microwave at HIGH (10) 2 to 3 minutes until tender. Add bacon, onion, garlic powder, salt and pepper. Microwave at HIGH (10) 1 to 2 minutes until heated through. Prepare Basic Omelet. Fill prepared omelet with garlic-potato mixture and fold over to serve.

Total Microwave Cooking Time 3 to 5 Minutes
Makes 1 serving

Asparagus Egg Roll-Up With Cheese Sauce

1 (10 oz.) pkg. frozen
  asparagus spears
6 tablespoons butter,
  melted
¾ cup all-purpose flour
3 cups milk
1 teaspoon dry mustard
½ teaspoon salt
4 eggs, separated
⅓ cup half & half
1 cup Swiss cheese,
  shredded

Grease and flour a 15x10x1-inch jelly roll pan. Line pan with wax paper, allowing paper to extend beyond the ends of the pan. Grease the wax paper with vegetable shortening, and dust lightly with flour. Set aside. Place asparagus in 1 ½ -quart casserole. Cover. Microwave at HIGH (10) 4 to 6 minutes; rearrange asparagus after 3 minutes. Drain. Cut asparagus into ½ -inch pieces. Set aside. Place melted butter in 2-quart casserole; add flour and stir until smooth. Microwave at HIGH (10) 1 minute. Gradually add milk to hot mixture, stirring constantly with a wire whisk. Microwave at HIGH (10) 5 to 6 minutes, until mixture is thickened, stirring every minute. Add dry mustard and salt. Set aside 1 cup of white sauce mixture. Place egg yolks in large mixing bowl and beat slightly. Gradually blend in remaining white sauce mixture. In medium bowl, beat egg whites at high speed until stiff peaks form. Fold egg whites into egg yolk mixture. Spoon mixture into jelly roll pan, spreading evenly. Place metal accessory rack on floor of oven. Preheat oven to 325°F. Convection Bake 40 to 45 minutes until puffed and firm; turn pan after 20 minutes. Loosen edges around pan. Invert jelly roll pan on wax paper. Remove pan, peel off wax paper. Allow oven to cool before using microwave.

In medium mixing bowl, combine half & half, Swiss cheese and reserved white sauce. Microwave at HIGH (10) 4 to 5 minutes until cheese is melted and sauce is smooth. Stir after 2 minutes. Spread ¾ cup cheese sauce over roll. Top with asparagus. Starting at narrow end, carefully roll into jelly roll, using wax paper for support. Top with remaining cheese sauce.

Total Convection Cooking Time 40 to 45 Minutes
Makes 8 servings

Invert from jelly roll pan onto wax paper.

Using wax paper as support, carefully roll into jelly roll.

Cheese Rarebit

8 oz. pasteurized
  processed cheese, diced
1 tablespoon butter
¼ teaspoon salt
¼ teaspoon dry mustard
½ teaspoon
  Worcestershire sauce
Dash cayenne pepper
¼ cup half & half
1 egg yolk, beaten

In 1-quart casserole, place cheese and butter. Microwave at HIGH (10) 2 minutes, until smooth, stirring every minute. Add salt, mustard, Worcestershire sauce and cayenne pepper. Quickly stir in half & half and egg yolk. Microwave at MEDIUM (5) 4 to 5 minutes, until hot, stirring every minute. Serve over toast.

Total Microwave Cooking Time 6 to 7 Minutes
Makes 3 to 4 servings

Eggs & Cheese

▲ *Ham and Egg Casserole*

Ham and Egg Casserole

**3 cups white bread cubes,
 crusts removed**
**2 cups sharp Cheddar
 cheese, shredded**
**¼ cup green onion,
 finely chopped**
**1 (4 ½ oz.) can sliced
 mushrooms**
**1 cup ham, cut into
 ½-inch cubes**
4 eggs
½ cup milk
1 teaspoon dry mustard
⅛ teaspoon pepper
Dash hot sauce

In 2-quart oblong baking dish, place cubed bread. Sprinkle cheese, green onion and mushrooms over bread. Top with ham cubes. In small mixing bowl, beat together eggs, milk, dry mustard, pepper and hot sauce. Pour egg mixture over bread, cheese and ham. Cover with wax paper. Microwave at HIGH (10) 3 to 4 minutes. Rotate dish ½ turn. Microwave at MEDIUM (5) 7 to 9 minutes. Let stand 5 minutes before serving.

TO COOK BY COMBINATION: Place metal accessory rack on floor of oven. Preheat oven to 350°F. Cook on Combination 22 to 27 minutes, uncovered, until knife inserted in center comes out clean. Let stand 5 minutes before serving.

TO COOK BY CONVECTION: Place metal accessory rack on floor of oven. Preheat oven to 350°F. Convection Bake 30 to 35 minutes, uncovered, until knife inserted in center comes out clean.

Total Microwave Cooking Time 10 to 13 Minutes
Total Combination Cooking Time 22 to 27 Minutes
Total Convection Cooking Time 30 to 35 Minutes
Makes 4 to 6 servings

Corn and Cheese Souffle

¼ cup butter, melted
¼ cup all-purpose flour
¼ teaspoon salt
⅛ teaspoon white pepper
1 ½ cups milk
2 ¼ cups Cheddar cheese, shredded
1 (8 oz.) can whole kernel corn, drained
6 eggs, separated

In 1 ½-quart casserole, combine melted butter, flour, salt and pepper. Gradually stir in milk. Microwave at MEDIUM HIGH (7) 4 to 6 minutes, until slightly thickened, stirring every 2 minutes. Add cheese and corn. Microwave at MEDIUM HIGH (7) 2 minutes; stir to blend. In small mixing bowl, beat egg yolks. Stir in a small amount of cheese sauce; return yolk mixture to sauce, blending well. Cool slightly.

Place metal accessory rack on floor of oven. Preheat oven to 350°F. In medium mixing bowl, beat egg whites until soft peaks form. With a rubber spatula, fold egg whites into cheese sauce just until blended. Pour into greased 2-quart souffle dish. Cook on Combination 18 to 23 minutes until top is puffed and golden and center is set. Serve immediately.

Total Combination Cooking Time 18 to 23 Minutes
Makes 4 servings

Beat egg whites until soft peaks form.

Pepper Cheese Pastry

2 tablespoons olive oil
1 medium onion, thinly sliced
½ cup sweet red pepper, cut into 2-inch thin strips
½ cup green pepper, cut into 2-inch thin strips
½ teaspoon hot sauce
2 (8 oz.) pkgs. crescent rolls
½ cup grated Parmesan cheese
1 lb. Monterey Jack cheese, shredded

In 2-quart casserole, combine oil, onion and peppers. Microwave at HIGH (10) 6 to 7 minutes, stirring every 2 minutes. Add hot sauce. Place metal accessory rack on floor of oven. Preheat oven to 350°F. Grease a 15x10x1-inch jelly roll pan. Press crescent roll dough onto jelly roll pan. Bake for 5 minutes. Sprinkle with Parmesan cheese. Top with onion, peppers and Monterey Jack cheese. Convection Bake 25 to 30 minutes until cheese begins to brown.

Total Convection Cooking Time 30 to 35 Minutes
Makes 8 servings

Gently fold egg whites into cheese sauce to blend.

Swiss Cheese Fondue

4 cups Swiss cheese, shredded
¼ cup all-purpose flour
⅛ teaspoon garlic powder
⅛ teaspoon pepper
Dash nutmeg
1 cup white wine
2 tablespoons Kirsch, optional
French bread, cut into cubes, or bread sticks

In medium mixing bowl, toss cheese with flour, garlic, pepper and nutmeg. In 2-quart casserole, add wine. Microwave at HIGH (10) 2 to 3 minutes. Gradually add 2 cups of cheese; stir until smooth. Microwave at MEDIUM (5) 2 to 3 minutes; stir after 1 minute. Add remaining cheese and Kirsch; stir until smooth. Microwave at MEDIUM (5) 3 to 4 minutes, until cheese is melted; stir after 1 minute. Serve hot with French bread.

Total Microwave Cooking Time 7 to 10 Minutes
Makes 6 servings

Eggs & Cheese

▲ *Vegetable Frittata*

Vegetable Frittata

2 tablespoons butter
1 small onion, sliced
4 asparagus tips, sliced
3 mushrooms, sliced
½ small zucchini, sliced
8 eggs, beaten
½ cup milk
¼ teaspoon salt
⅛ teaspoon pepper
Dash hot sauce

Place butter and onion in 9-inch quiche dish. Microwave at HIGH (10) 2 to 3 minutes. Add asparagus, mushrooms and zucchini. Microwave at HIGH (10) 4 to 5 minutes; stir after 2 minutes. In small mixing bowl, combine eggs, milk, salt, pepper and hot sauce. Pour over vegetables.

Place metal accessory rack on floor of oven. Preheat oven to 325°F. Convection Bake 25 to 30 minutes until set.

Total Convection Cooking Time 25 to 30 Minutes
Makes 2 to 4 servings

Breakfast Cheese Pizza

Arrange sliced bread buttered side down to form crust.

3 green onions, chopped
1 tablespoon bacon
   drippings
½ cup fresh mushrooms,
   finely chopped
5 slices bread, buttered
Garlic salt
1 cup Cheddar cheese,
   shredded
1 cup Swiss cheese,
   shredded
2 tablespoons all-purpose
   flour
6 slices bacon, cooked
   and crumbled
1½ cups milk
2 eggs
¼ teaspoon salt
¼ teaspoon pepper

In 2-quart casserole, combine onions, bacon drippings and mushrooms. Microwave at HIGH (10) 2 to 3 minutes until onions are transparent and mushrooms are tender. Set aside. Sprinkle buttered bread with garlic salt. Cut slices in half diagonally. Arrange, buttered side down, in 10-inch pie plate, forming a crust. Sprinkle onions and mushrooms over bread.

In medium mixing bowl, combine Cheddar cheese, Swiss cheese, flour and bacon. Spread over top of onions and mushrooms. In small mixing bowl, beat together milk, eggs, salt and pepper. Pour evenly over cheese. Microwave at MEDIUM HIGH (7) 12 to 15 minutes until knife inserted in center comes out clean.

TO COOK BY CONVECTION: Place metal accessory rack on floor of oven. Preheat oven to 350°F. Convection Bake 30 to 40 minutes.

Total Microwave Cooking Time 14 to 18 Minutes
Total Convection Cooking Time 30 to 40 Minutes
Makes 6 to 8 servings

Spinach Quiche

1 tablespoon butter
1 ¾ cups fresh mushrooms, sliced
1 (12 oz.) pkg. frozen spinach souffle, thawed
½ lb. sweet Italian sausage, casings removed, cooked and crumbled
¾ cup Swiss cheese, shredded
2 eggs, beaten
3 tablespoons whipping cream
½ teaspoon pepper
½ teaspoon hot sauce
1 (9-inch) deep-dish pie crust, baked

In 2-quart casserole, combine butter and mushrooms. Microwave at HIGH (10) 3 to 4 minutes until mushrooms are tender. Drain well. Add spinach souffle, sausage, cheese, eggs, cream, pepper and hot sauce. Pour into crust. Microwave at MEDIUM HIGH (7) 16 to 20 minutes, until center is set, but not dry. Let stand 5 minutes to complete cooking.

TO COOK BY COMBINATION: Place metal accessory rack on floor of oven. Preheat oven to 350°F. Cook on Combination 20 to 25 minutes. Let stand 5 to 10 minutes to firm before serving.

TO COOK BY CONVECTION: Place metal accessory rack on floor of oven. Preheat oven to 350°F. Convection Bake 25 to 35 minutes until knife inserted in center comes out clean. Let stand 5 to 10 minutes before serving.

> Total Microwave Cooking Time 19 to 24 Minutes
> Total Combination Cooking Time 20 to 25 Minutes
> Total Convection Cooking Time 25 to 35 Minutes
> Makes 6 servings

Test for doneness by inserting knife in center. Knife should come out clean.

Ham & Grits Quiche

1 tablespoon butter
½ cup fresh mushrooms, chopped
¼ cup onion, chopped
½ cup milk
½ cup whipping cream
4 eggs, beaten
½ teaspoon dry mustard
¼ teaspoon pepper
¼ teaspoon nutmeg
½ cup Swiss cheese, shredded
½ cup Cheddar cheese, shredded
1 (9-inch) deep dish pie crust, baked
¾ cup cooked ham, chopped
4 sausage links, chopped and cooked
3 bacon slices, chopped and cooked
½ cup quick cooking grits, cooked

In 2-quart casserole, combine butter, mushrooms and onion. Microwave at HIGH (10) 3 to 4 minutes until mushrooms are tender and onion is transparent. Set aside. In medium mixing bowl, combine milk, whipping cream, eggs, dry mustard, pepper and nutmeg. Set aside.

In separate mixing bowl, combine Swiss cheese and Cheddar cheese. Sprinkle ham and sausage over bottom of crust. Top with half of cheese and all of bacon. Pour mushroom mixture over bacon. Add grits. Sprinkle with remaining cheese. Pour cream mixture over cheese. Microwave at MEDIUM HIGH (7) 16 to 20 minutes until center is set, but not dry. Let stand 5 minutes before serving.

TO COOK BY COMBINATION: Place metal accessory rack on floor of oven. Preheat oven to 350°F. Cook on Combination 25 to 30 minutes. Let stand 5 to 10 minutes before serving.

TO COOK BY CONVECTION: Place metal accessory rack on floor of oven. Preheat oven to 350°F. Convection Bake 40 to 45 minutes until knife inserted in center comes out clean. Let stand 10 minutes before serving.

> Total Microwave Cooking Time 19 to 24 Minutes
> Total Combination Cooking Time 25 to 30 Minutes
> Total Convection Cooking Time 40 to 45 Minutes
> Makes 6 servings

Sauces

Raisin Sauce

½ cup orange juice
½ cup water
1 tablespoon cornstarch
1 tablespoon rum, optional
½ cup raisins
⅓ cup currant jelly*
Dash allspice

In 1½-quart casserole, stir together orange juice, water and cornstarch until blended. Stir in rum, raisins, currant jelly and allspice. Microwave at HIGH (10) 9 to 11 minutes, until sauce is thickened, stirring every 2 minutes.

*Substitution: Use pineapple or apricot preserves for currant jelly.

Total Microwave Cooking Time 9 to 11 Minutes
Makes 1½ cups

Barbecue Sauce

2 tablespoons butter
1 small onion, grated
1 cup catsup
⅓ cup white vinegar
4 tablespoons Worcestershire sauce
½ cup brown sugar, packed
⅛ teaspoon garlic powder
¼ teaspoon seasoned salt
2 teaspoons pepper
1 tablespoon chili powder

In 2-quart casserole, place butter and onion. Microwave at HIGH (10) 2 to 3 minutes until onion is tender. Add catsup, vinegar, Worcestershire sauce, brown sugar, garlic powder, seasoned salt, pepper and chili powder. Microwave at HIGH (10) 5 minutes. Stir and continue to Microwave at MEDIUM HIGH (7) 8 to 10 minutes, until sauce is thickened, stirring every 3 minutes.

Total Microwave Cooking Time 15 to 18 Minutes
Makes 2 cups

Homemade Special Spaghetti Sauce

2 tablespoons oil
¾ cup onion, chopped
2 cloves garlic, finely chopped
1 (28 oz.) can whole tomatoes, chopped
1 (6 oz.) can tomato paste
½ cup water
1 bay leaf, crushed
½ teaspoon salt
¼ teaspoon basil
¼ teaspoon oregano

In 3-quart casserole, combine oil, onion and garlic. Microwave at HIGH (10) 1 to 2 minutes. Add tomatoes, tomato paste, water, bay leaf, salt, basil and oregano. Cover with wax paper. Microwave at HIGH (10) 6 to 7 minutes; stir after 3 minutes. Continue to Microwave at MEDIUM (5) 1 hour, stirring every 10 minutes.

Meat Sauce: Add ½ pound ground beef or sausage, cooked and drained.

Total Microwave Cooking Time 1 hour 7 Minutes to 1 hour 9 Minutes
Makes 1½ quarts

Hot Bacon Sauce

3 tablespoons sugar
3 teaspoons cornstarch
6 tablespoons white vinegar
¼ cup water
6 slices bacon, chopped and cooked, reserve drippings
1 green onion, chopped

In 1½-quart casserole, combine sugar, cornstarch, vinegar, water and bacon drippings. Microwave at HIGH (10) 3 to 5 minutes, until sauce thickens; stir after 2 minutes. Stir in bacon and onion. Serve over blanched vegetables, or as a dressing for potato salad or spinach salad.

Total Microwave Cooking Time 3 to 5 Minutes
Makes 1 cup

◀ Raisin Sauce

Sauces

Basic White Sauce

**2 tablespoons butter,
melted**
**2 tablespoons all-purpose
flour**
¼ teaspoon salt
1 cup milk

In 1½-quart casserole, combine melted butter, flour and salt. Gradually add milk; stir until smooth. Microwave at MEDIUM (5) 3 to 5 minutes, until sauce is thickened, stirring every minute with a wire whisk.

Cheese Sauce: Stir in ½ to ¾ cup shredded cheese. Microwave at MEDIUM (5) 1 minute, if necessary, to completely melt cheese.
Curry Sauce: Stir in 1 to 2 teaspoons curry powder.
Horseradish Sauce: Stir in 1 tablespoon prepared horseradish.

> **Total Microwave Cooking Time 3 to 5 Minutes**
> **Makes 1 cup**

To make a cheese sauce, add shredded cheese to the Basic White Sauce recipe.

Red Clam Sauce

½ teaspoon olive oil
1 clove garlic, minced
**2 (6½-oz.) cans minced
clams**
2 (8-oz.) cans tomato sauce
2 tablespoons tomato paste
**2 tablespoons fresh parsley,
snipped**
**2 tablespoons onion,
chopped**
**2 tablespoons grated
Parmesan cheese**
½ teaspoon basil
½ teaspoon oregano
**⅛ teaspoon freshly ground
pepper**

In 2-quart casserole, combine olive oil and garlic. Microwave at MEDIUM HIGH (7) 1 to 2 minutes. Drain clams, reserving juice from one can. Set clams aside.

In small mixing bowl, combine clam juice, tomato sauce, tomato paste, parsley, onion, Parmesan cheese, basil, oregano and pepper. Cover and Microwave at MEDIUM HIGH (7) 10 to 12 minutes. Stir in clams and Microwave at HIGH (10) 2 to 3 minutes. Serve over pasta.

> **Total Microwave Cooking Time 13 to 17 Minutes**
> **Makes 3 cups**

White Clam Sauce

2 tablespoons butter
**1 tablespoon onion, finely
chopped**
**2 (6½-oz.) cans minced
clams**
⅛ teaspoon garlic juice
¼ cup dry white wine
⅔ cup whipping cream
**2 tablespoons fresh parsley,
snipped**
¼ teaspoon oregano
**¼ teaspoon lemon peel,
grated**
⅛ teaspoon salt
⅛ teaspoon pepper

In 1½-quart casserole, place butter and onion. Microwave at HIGH (10) 2 to 3 minutes. Drain clams, reserving juice from one can. Add clams, clam juice, garlic juice, white wine, whipping cream, parsley, oregano, lemon peel, salt and pepper. Stir to blend. Cover and Microwave at HIGH (10) 4 to 6 minutes, stirring every minute. Serve over pasta.

> **Total Microwave Cooking Time 6 to 9 Minutes**
> **Makes 2 cups**

▲ *Vanilla Sauce*

Vanilla Sauce

⅓ cup sugar
1½ tablespoons cornstarch
1 cup milk
1 tablespoon butter
1 teaspoon vanilla

In 1-quart casserole, combine sugar and cornstarch. Add milk, stirring constantly with a wire whisk until smooth. Microwave at HIGH (10) 3 to 5 minutes, until sauce is thickened, stirring every minute with a wire whisk. Blend in butter and vanilla. Refrigerate for 30 minutes.

Total Microwave Cooking Time 3 to 5 Minutes
Makes 1½ cups

Hot Fudge Sauce

1 cup (6 oz.) semisweet chocolate pieces
½ cup light corn syrup
¼ cup half & half or milk
1 tablespoon butter
1 teaspoon vanilla

In 1½-quart casserole, combine chocolate and syrup. Microwave at MEDIUM HIGH (7) 5 to 6 minutes, stirring every 2 minutes. Gradually add half & half; stir until smooth. Blend in butter and vanilla.

Total Microwave Cooking Time 5 to 6 Minutes
Makes 1½ cups

Brandied Cherry Sauce

1 (17 oz.) can dark sweet pitted cherries in heavy syrup
½ cup sugar
1½ tablespoons cornstarch
1 cup water
¼ cup brandy

Drain cherries, reserving ¼ cup syrup. In 1-quart casserole, combine sugar and cornstarch. Add cherries, syrup and water, stirring until smooth. Microwave at HIGH (10) 3 to 4 minutes, until sauce is thickened, stirring every minute. Spoon cherries over dessert. Microwave brandy in 1-cup glass measure at HIGH (10) 30 to 45 seconds. Remove one tablespoon brandy into metal spoon. Pour remaining brandy over cherries. Ignite brandy in spoon and pour over cherries to flame.

Total Microwave Cooking Time 3½ to 4¾ Minutes
Makes 1½ cups

To flame, carefully ignite warmed brandy in spoon and pour over fruit.

Vegetables

Acorn Squash with Cranberry Filling

2 medium acorn squash
  (about 2-lbs.)
1 (16 oz.) can cranberry
  sauce
1 tablespoon honey
¼ teaspoon allspice

Prick squash several times with fork to allow steam to escape. Place in oven. Microwave at HIGH (10) 16 to 22 minutes until soft when pricked with fork. Turn squash over and rearrange after 9 minutes. Let stand 5 minutes. Cut in half and remove seeds. Place cut side up in 10-in. pie plate.

In small bowl, combine cranberry sauce, honey and allspice. Microwave at HIGH (10) 4 to 5 minutes until hot and bubbly; stir after 2 minutes. Spoon into squash halves. Microwave at HIGH (10) 3 to 4 minutes until heated through.

Total Microwave Cooking Time 23 to 31 Minutes
Makes 4 servings

Stir Fry Vegetables

1 tablespoon oil
1 tablespoon butter
2 tablespoons soy sauce
¼ teaspoon garlic powder
3 medium onions,
  quartered lengthwise
1 medium green pepper,
  cut in ¼ -inch strips
2 cups cabbage,
  thinly sliced
⅔ cup carrots, sliced
  diagonally
¼ cup green onions, sliced
1 cup broccoli flowerets
1 cup cauliflower flowerets
2 stalks celery,
  sliced diagonally

In 3-quart casserole, place oil, butter, soy sauce and garlic powder. Microwave at HIGH (10) 1 to 2 minutes until hot. Add onions, green pepper, cabbage, carrots, green onions, broccoli, cauliflower and celery. Toss to coat. Cover. Microwave at HIGH (10) 12 to 15 minutes; stir after 6 minutes. Serve immediately.

Total Microwave Cooking Time 13 to 17 Minutes
Makes 6 to 8 servings

Zesty Tomatoes & Squash

2 tablespoons butter,
  melted
⅛ teaspoon garlic powder
1 teaspoon oregano
½ teaspoon basil
½ teaspoon seasoned salt
⅛ teaspoon pepper
2 medium zucchini,
  thinly sliced
1 medium yellow squash,
  thinly sliced
2 small tomatoes, each cut
  into 4 wedges

In 2-quart casserole, combine butter, garlic powder, oregano, basil, seasoned salt and pepper. Add zucchini and yellow squash. Toss to coat. Cover. Microwave at HIGH (10) 8 to 10 minutes, until vegetables are tender; stir after 5 minutes. Add tomatoes. Cover; let stand 2 minutes.

Total Microwave Cooking Time 8 to 10 Minutes
Makes 4 servings

Vegetables

▲ *Asparagus with Mustard Dressing*

Arrange with tips to the center of dish.

Asparagus with Mustard Dressing

½ cup mayonnaise
2 tablespoons onion, finely chopped
1 tablespoon white wine
2 teaspoons prepared mustard
½ teaspoon soy sauce
⅛ teaspoon ground ginger
⅛ teaspoon white pepper
1 lb. fresh asparagus
¼ cup water

In 2-cup glass measure, combine mayonnaise, onion, wine, mustard, soy sauce, ginger and pepper. Mix well and refrigerate.

Arrange asparagus in 2-quart oblong glass baking dish with thicker pieces to outside of dish and tips to center. Add water; cover with plastic wrap, turning back one corner to vent. Microwave at HIGH (10) 2 to 3 minutes until crisp-tender. Drain and chill.

Arrange asparagus spears on serving platter. Top with mustard dressing.

Total Microwave Cooking Time 2 to 3 Minutes
Makes 3 to 4 servings

Sauteed Mushrooms

1 lb. fresh mushrooms, sliced
¼ cup butter
3 tablespoons red wine vinegar
¼ teaspoon garlic salt

In 2-quart casserole, combine mushrooms, butter, wine vinegar and garlic salt. Cover. Microwave at HIGH (10) 8 to 10 minutes, until mushrooms are tender; stir after 4 minutes.

Total Microwave Cooking Time 8 to 10 Minutes
Makes 4 servings

Asparagus and Cheese Brunch

8 slices bread
1 (16 oz.) can asparagus, drained, cut into 2-inch pieces
2 cups Cheddar cheese, shredded
4 eggs, beaten
2 ½ cups milk
2 tablespoons onion, minced
½ teaspoon salt
⅛ teaspoon pepper
¼ teaspoon dry mustard
¼ teaspoon paprika
2 tablespoons butter, melted

Remove crusts from bread and cut into cubes. In 1 ½-quart oblong glass baking dish, arrange half the bread. Cover with asparagus and sprinkle with Cheddar cheese. Cover with remaining bread. In 4-cup glass measure, combine eggs, milk, onion, salt, pepper, mustard, paprika and butter. Pour mixture over casserole. Let stand 20 minutes. Cover with wax paper. Microwave at MEDIUM HIGH (7) 12 to 15 minutes until knife inserted in center comes out clean.

TO COOK BY COMBINATION: Place metal accessory rack on floor of oven. Preheat oven to 350°F. Cook on Combination 25 to 30 minutes until puffed and lightly browned.

TO COOK BY CONVECTION: Place metal accessory rack on floor of oven. Preheat oven to 350°F. Convection Bake 45 to 50 minutes until puffed and lightly browned.

Total Microwave Cooking Time 12 to 15 Minutes
Total Combination Cooking Time 25 to 30 Minutes
Total Convection Cooking Time 45 to 50 Minutes
Makes 6 servings

Corn Pudding

2 tablespoons butter, melted
2 tablespoons all-purpose flour
2 tablespoons sugar
½ teaspoon salt
1 cup milk
3 eggs, beaten
1 (17 oz.) can whole kernel corn, drained

In 1 ½-quart casserole, combine butter, flour, sugar, salt, milk, eggs and corn. Microwave at HIGH (10) 14 to 16 minutes until center is barely set.

TO COOK BY COMBINATION: Place metal accessory rack on floor of oven. Preheat oven to 350°F. Cook on Combination 22 to 27 minutes until center is barely set.

TO COOK BY CONVECTION: Place metal accessory rack on floor of oven. Preheat oven to 350°F. Convection Bake 35 to 40 minutes until center is barely set.

Total Microwave Cooking Time 14 to 16 Minutes
Total Combination Cooking Time 22 to 27 Minutes
Total Convection Cooking Time 35 to 40 Minutes
Makes 4 to 6 servings

Sweet & Sour Beets

3 tablespoons butter, melted
2 large fresh beets, peeled and grated
2 teaspoons cornstarch
¼ cup water
⅛ teaspoon salt
1 tablespoon vinegar
3 tablespoons sugar

In 2-quart casserole, combine butter and grated beets. Cover. Microwave at MEDIUM (5) 9 to 11 minutes; stir after 5 minutes. In small mixing bowl, dissolve cornstarch in water. Add cornstarch, salt, vinegar and sugar to beets. Mix well. Cover. Microwave at HIGH (10) 3 to 5 minutes; stir after 2 minutes.

Total Microwave Cooking Time 12 to 16 Minutes
Makes 4 to 6 servings

Vegetables

Cabbage Rolls

Cooked cabbage leaves should be soft and pliable.

Wrap leaf around meat mixture and secure with toothpick.

**8 whole, fresh cabbage
  leaves**
½ cup water
1 lb. ground chuck
½ cup instant rice
**3 tablespoons onion,
  finely chopped**
**3 tablespoons green
  pepper, finely chopped**
½ teaspoon salt
⅛ teaspoon pepper
⅛ teaspoon nutmeg
½ cup tomato juice
1 (15 oz.) can tomato sauce
**3 tablespoons brown
  sugar, firmly packed**
1 tablespoon lemon juice
**1 tablespoon
  Worcestershire sauce**
½ teaspoon garlic salt

In 3-quart casserole, place cabbage leaves and water. Cover. Microwave at HIGH (10) 7 to 9 minutes until leaves are soft and pliable. In medium size mixing bowl, combine ground chuck, rice, onion, green pepper, salt, pepper and nutmeg. Divide into 8 portions and place one portion on each of the partially-cooked cabbage leaves. Roll leaf around meat mixture. Secure with a toothpick. Place rolls, seam-side down in 3-quart casserole.

In small bowl, blend tomato juice, tomato sauce, brown sugar, lemon juice, Worcestershire sauce and garlic salt. Pour over cabbage rolls. Cover. Microwave at HIGH (10) 15 to 18 minutes. Rotate dish ½ turn and baste rolls with sauce after 7 minutes. Let stand, covered, 5 minutes before serving.

TO COOK BY COMBINATION: Place metal accessory rack on floor of oven. Preheat oven to 350°F. Cook on Combination 22 to 26 minutes. Baste rolls with sauce after 10 minutes.

TO COOK BY CONVECTION: Place metal accessory rack on floor of oven. Preheat oven to 350°F. Convection Bake 30 to 35 minutes. Baste rolls with sauce every 15 minutes.

> Total Microwave Cooking Time 22 to 27 Minutes
> Total Combination Cooking Time 22 to 26 Minutes
> Total Convection Cooking Time 30 to 35 Minutes
> Makes 4 servings

Delicious Yams

**1 (30 oz.) can yams,
  well drained**
⅓ cup orange juice
1 tablespoon cornstarch
**½ cup brown sugar,
  firmly packed**
**2 tablespoons butter,
  melted**
**½ cup walnuts, coarsely
  chopped**
**2 teaspoons grated
  orange rind**
**⅓ cup shredded coconut,
  toasted**

Arrange yams in 1½-quart casserole. In medium bowl, combine orange juice and cornstarch; stir until cornstarch is completely dissolved. Blend in brown sugar and butter. Add walnuts and orange rind; pour over yams. Microwave at HIGH (10) 10 to 12 minutes. Sprinkle with toasted coconut before serving.

TO COOK BY COMBINATION: Place metal accessory rack on floor of oven. Preheat oven to 350°F. Cook on Combination 17 to 20 minutes. Sprinkle with toasted coconut before serving.

TO COOK BY CONVECTION: Place metal accessory rack on floor of oven. Preheat oven to 350°F. Convection Bake 20 to 25 minutes. Sprinkle with toasted coconut before serving.

> Total Microwave Cooking Time 10 to 12 Minutes
> Total Combination Cooking Time 17 to 20 Minutes
> Total Convection Cooking Time 20 to 25 Minutes
> Makes 6 servings

▲ *Cabbage Rolls*

Scalloped Potatoes

¼ **cup butter, melted**
¼ **cup all-purpose flour**
2 **cups milk**
1 **tablespoon dried onion flakes**
½ **teaspoon salt**
¼ **teaspoon pepper**
6 **medium potatoes, peeled and thinly sliced**
Paprika

In 4-cup glass measure, combine melted butter and flour; gradually add milk, stirring until smooth. Add onion flakes, salt and pepper. Microwave at MEDIUM HIGH (7) 7 to 9 minutes, until sauce is smooth and slightly thickened, stirring every 3 minutes. In 2-quart casserole, alternately layer potatoes and sauce. Cover. Microwave at MEDIUM HIGH (7) 25 to 30 minutes until potatoes are tender. Sprinkle with paprika. Let stand, covered, 5 minutes.

TO COOK BY COMBINATION: Place metal accessory rack on floor of oven. Preheat oven to 350°F. Cook on Combination 35 to 40 minutes.

Total Microwave Cooking Time 32 to 39 Minutes
Total Combination Cooking Time 35 to 40 Minutes
Makes 6 servings

German Potato Salad

6 **medium potatoes, peeled and thinly sliced**
¼ **cup water**
6 **slices bacon, cooked, reserve drippings**
½ **cup green onion, chopped**
2 **tablespoons all-purpose flour**
1 **tablespoon sugar**
½ **teaspoon salt**
⅛ **teaspoon pepper**
¼ **teaspoon celery seed**
½ **cup water**
⅓ **cup vinegar**

In 2-quart casserole, place potatoes and ¼ cup water. Cover with vented plastic wrap. Microwave at HIGH (10) 10 to 15 minutes; stir after 5 minutes. Let stand, covered, 5 minutes.

In 1½-quart casserole, combine bacon drippings and onion. Microwave at HIGH (10) 2 to 3 minutes until onion is transparent. Stir in flour, sugar, salt, pepper, celery seed, water and vinegar. Microwave at HIGH (10) 3 to 4 minutes; stir after 2 minutes. Crumble bacon over potatoes. Pour liquid over potatoes and bacon, mixing well.

Total Microwave Cooking Time 15 to 22 Minutes
Makes 6 servings

Vegetables

▲ *Stuffed Yellow Squash*

Scoop out pulp and seeds leaving ¼-inch thick shell.

Stuffed Yellow Squash

3 large yellow squash
¼ lb. hot bulk sausage
½ cup green pepper, chopped
¼ cup onion, chopped
1 medium tomato, chopped
½ cup grated Parmesan cheese
1 cup mozzarella cheese, shredded

Cut squash in half, lengthwise. Scoop out pulp and seeds and discard, leaving ¼-inch thick shell. Set aside. In 2-quart casserole, combine sausage, onion and green pepper. Cover. Microwave at MEDIUM HIGH (7) 3 to 5 minutes, until sausage is brown; stir every 2 minutes. Drain. Add tomato and Parmesan cheese. Stir until well blended.

Spoon mixture into squash shells; place squash in 3-quart oblong glass baking dish. Cover with wax paper. Microwave at HIGH (10) 15 to 18 minutes; rotate dish ½ turn after 8 minutes. Sprinkle with mozzarella cheese. Microwave at HIGH (10) 2 to 3 minutes until cheese is melted.

Total Microwave Cooking Time 20 to 26 Minutes
Makes 6 servings

Golden Stuffed Artichokes

4 medium artichokes
1 cup water
½ teaspoon salt
**1 (6 oz.) pkg. chicken-
flavor range top
stuffing mix with
crumbs**
1½ cups water
¼ cup butter
2 small carrots, grated
1 small onion, diced
1 tablespoon olive oil
**1 (3 ¼ oz.) pkg. salted
cashews**

Prepare artichokes by discarding the tough outer leaves.
Snip tips off leaves with scissors and cut off stems.
In 3-quart casserole, place artichokes, water and salt.
Cover. Microwave at HIGH (10) 12 to 14 minutes.
Remove artichokes and place upside down to partially
cool. In 1 ½-quart casserole, combine vegetable
seasoning packet from stuffing mix, water and butter.
Cover. Microwave at HIGH (10) 4 to 5 minutes. Stir
crumbs into mixture just to moisten. Cover and let
stand. In 1-quart casserole, combine carrots, onion and
oil. Cover. Microwave at HIGH (10) 3 to 4 minutes until
vegetables are tender. Add carrot mixture and cashews
to bread stuffing.

Force the center of each artichoke open to form a well.
Remove the center leaves and the choke (the fuzzy,
purple-tinged area covering the heart, or base of the
artichoke) with a spoon. Stuff artichokes with cashew-
carrot stuffing. Rearrange in 3-quart casserole. Microwave at HIGH (10) 4 to 6 minutes until heated through.

Total Microwave Cooking Time 23 to 29 Minutes
Makes 4 stuffed artichokes

*After initial cooking, turn arti-
chokes upside down to partially
cool.*

Three Bean Bake

**¼ lb. bacon, cooked,
crumbled, reserve
drippings**
⅓ cup red onion, chopped
**¼ cup brown sugar,
firmly packed**
1 tablespoon cider vinegar
1 teaspoon dry mustard
1 (16 oz.) can pork & beans
**1 (15 ½ oz.) can kidney
beans, drained**
**1 (17 oz.) can lima beans,
drained**

In 3-quart oblong glass baking dish, combine bacon
drippings and onion. Microwave at HIGH (10) 2 to 3
minutes until onion is transparent. Add brown sugar,
vinegar, mustard, pork and beans, kidney beans, lima
beans and crumbled bacon. Stir well. Microwave at
HIGH (10) 10 to 12 minutes; stir after 6 minutes.

TO COOK BY COMBINATION: Place metal accessory rack on floor of oven. Preheat oven to 350°F. Cook
on Combination 20 to 25 minutes.

TO COOK BY CONVECTION: Place metal accessory
rack on floor of oven. Preheat oven to 350°F.
Convection Bake 30 to 35 minutes.

Total Microwave Cooking Time 12 to 15 Minutes
Total Combination Cooking Time 20 to 25 Minutes
Total Convection Cooking Time 30 to 35 Minutes
Makes 6 to 8 servings

*Open the center of each artichoke to
form a well. Remove the center
leaves and the choke (the area
covering the heart of the artichoke).*

Parmesan Cheese Potato Slices

**3 large baking potatoes,
sliced ¼ -inch thick**
**½ cup grated Parmesan
cheese**
⅛ teaspoon paprika
**3 tablespoons butter,
melted**

Place metal accessory rack on floor of oven. Preheat
oven to 350°F. Place sliced potatoes on metal baking
sheet. In 1-quart casserole, combine Parmesan cheese
and paprika. Brush potato slices with butter and
sprinkle with Parmesan cheese mixture. Convection
Bake 25 to 30 minutes.

Total Convection Cooking Time 25 to 30 Minutes
Makes 6 servings

*To eat, pull off leaves and dip in
melted butter or favorite sauce.*

Vegetables

Southern Stuffed Eggplant

1 medium eggplant
2 tablespoons water
¼ cup chopped onion
2 tablespoons butter
2 teaspoons parsley, snipped
1 (10 ½ oz.) can cream of mushroom soup
⅛ teaspoon pepper
1 teaspoon Worcestershire sauce
¾ cup butter cracker crumbs, divided
½ cup salted peanuts, coarsely chopped, optional
½ cup water
Paprika

Scoop out eggplant leaving the outer shell intact and dice the insides to be used in the stuffing.

Cut eggplant in half lengthwise. Scoop out insides leaving outer shell intact. Dice the scooped-out eggplant. In 2-quart casserole, combine diced eggplant and water. Cover. Microwave at HIGH (10) 6 to 8 minutes; stir after 3 minutes.

In 1½-quart casserole, place onion, butter and parsley. Microwave at HIGH (10) 2 to 3 minutes until onion is transparent.

Add onion mixture, soup, pepper, Worcestershire sauce, ½ cup cracker crumbs and peanuts to eggplant pieces. Evenly divide filling between the 2 shells. Place in 2-quart oblong glass baking dish. Add ½ cup water to dish. Cover with plastic wrap, turning back one corner to vent. Microwave at HIGH (10) 7 to 9 minutes until hot, rotating dish ½ turn after 3 minutes.

Sprinkle ¼ cup crumbs and paprika over top. Microwave at HIGH (10) 1 to 2 minutes until bubbly.

Total Microwave Cooking Time 16 to 22 Minutes
Makes 4 servings

Cheesy Broccoli

1 (10 oz.) pkg. frozen chopped broccoli
1 cup instant rice
1 (10 ¾ oz.) can cream of chicken soup
½ cup milk
1 (8 oz.) jar processed cheese spread
¼ teaspoon pepper
¼ cup onion, chopped
½ cup celery, chopped

Place broccoli in 2-quart casserole. Cover. Microwave at HIGH (10) 6 to 7 minutes. Drain. Set aside.

In 2-quart casserole, combine rice, soup, milk, cheese and pepper. Microwave at HIGH (10) 2 to 4 minutes until cheese melts and can be blended easily.

To cheese mixture, add onion, celery and broccoli. Stir thoroughly. Cover. Microwave at MEDIUM HIGH (7) 14 to 18 minutes; rotate dish ½ turn after 8 minutes. Remove cover for last 2 to 3 minutes of cooking. Let stand 5 minutes before serving.

Total Microwave Cooking Time 22 to 29 Minutes
Makes 6 servings

Twice Baked Potatoes

2 large baking potatoes, cooked according to chart on pg. 99
2 tablespoons butter
¼ cup milk
½ teaspoon salt
⅛ teaspoon pepper
¼ teaspoon garlic powder
½ cup Cheddar cheese, shredded

Cut cooked potatoes in half. Scoop out potatoes leaving ¼-inch thick shell. Set aside. In a medium mixing bowl, combine scooped out potato, butter, milk, salt, pepper and garlic powder. Whip potatoes with electric mixer at high speed for 1 minute, until smooth.

In an 8-inch square glass baking dish, place potato shells and fill with whipped potato mixture. Sprinkle Cheddar cheese on top. Microwave at HIGH (10) 2 to 3 minutes until cheese is melted and mixture is heated through.

Total Microwave Cooking Time 2 to 3 Minutes
Makes 2 servings

▲ *Wilted Spinach Salad*

Wilted Spinach Salad

3 strips bacon
¼ cup vinegar
2 teaspoons sugar
¼ teaspoon salt
⅛ teaspoon pepper
⅛ teaspoon dried tarragon
½ cup sliced celery
1 small red onion,
thinly sliced
1 pkg. of fresh spinach
leaves, torn (about
8 cups total)
2 medium oranges, peeled
and sliced*
⅓ cup cashews,
coarsely broken

In 3-quart casserole, snip bacon into 1-inch pieces. Cover with paper towel. Microwave at HIGH (10) 2 to 3 minutes, until crisp. With slotted spoon, place bacon on paper towels to drain.

To bacon drippings add vinegar, sugar, salt, pepper and tarragon. Microwave at HIGH (10) 2 to 3 minutes until mixture boils. Stir in celery and onion.

Gradually add spinach to hot dressing, tossing to coat each piece. Add crumbled bacon, orange segments and cashews. Toss again lightly. Serve immediately.

*Substitute 1 (11 oz.) can Mandarin oranges, drained.

Total Microwave Cooking Time 4 to 6 Minutes
Makes 8 to 10 servings

Vegetables

Vegetable Microwaving Guide

1. Salt vegetables after cooking. Salting before cooking may cause darkening and dried out spots.
2. Arrange vegetables, like asparagus, with the thickest pieces to the outside of the dish.
3. Use casserole lid to cover vegetables when cooking. When using plastic wrap, turn back corner to vent.
4. Size of vegetable pieces effects cooking time. Larger pieces take longer.
5. For more even heating, stirring or rotating vegetables during cooking is recommended.

VEGETABLE		Amount	Procedure / Comments	Power Level	Time, Minutes
Artichokes	Fresh	4 medium	In 3-quart casserole, place 1 cup water.	High (10)	15 to 18
Asparagus	Fresh Cuts	1-lb. (3 cups, cut into 1 to 2-inch pieces)	In 2-quart casserole, place ¼ cup water.	High (10)	8 to 10
	Spears	1-lb.	In 1½-quart oblong glass baking dish, place ¼ cup water.	Medium High (7)	8 to 10
	Frozen Spears	10-oz. pkg.	In 1-quart casserole.	High (10)	8 to 10
Beans	Fresh Green	1-lb., cut in half	In 1½-quart casserole, place ½ cup water.	High (10)	13 to 17
	Frozen Green	10-oz. pkg.	In 1-quart casserole, place 2 tablespoons water.	High (10)	6 to 8
	Frozen Lima	10-oz. pkg.	In 1-quart casserole, place ¼ cup water.	High (10)	6 to 8
Beets	Fresh Whole	1 bunch	In 2-quart casserole, place ½ cup water.	High (10)	20 to 25
Broccoli	Fresh Spears	1 bunch (1¼ to 1½-lbs.)	In 3-quart oblong glass baking dish, place ¼ cup water.	High (10)	12 to 15
	Cut	1 bunch (1¼ to 1½-lbs.)	In 2-quart casserole, place ½ cup water.	High (10)	10 to 12
	Frozen Chopped	10-oz. pkg.	In 1-quart casserole.	High (10)	6 to 8
	Spears	10-oz. pkg.	In 1-quart casserole, place 3 tablespoons water.	High (10)	6 to 8
Brussels Sprouts	Fresh	1-lb.	In 1½-quart casserole, place ¼ cup water.	High (10)	8 to 10
	Frozen	10-oz. pkg.	In 1-quart casserole, place 2 tablespoons water.	High (10)	7 to 9
Cabbage	Fresh	1 medium head (about 2-lbs.)	In 1½ or 2-quart casserole, place ¼ cup water.	High (10)	7 to 11
	Wedges		In 2 or 3-quart casserole, place ¼ cup water.	High (10)	14 to 18
Carrots	Fresh Sliced	1-lb.	In 1½-quart casserole, place ¼ cup water.	High (10)	7 to 11
	Frozen	10-oz. pkg.	In 1-quart casserole, place 2 tablespoons water.	High (10)	6 to 8
Cauliflower	Fresh Whole	1 medium head	In 1½-quart casserole, place ½ cup water.	High (10)	10 to 17
	Flowerets	1 medium head		High (10)	10 to 14
	Frozen	10-oz. pkg.	In 1-quart casserole, place 2 tablespoons water.	High (10)	6 to 8

VEGETABLE		Amount	Procedure / Comments	Power Level	Time, Minutes
Corn	**Frozen Kernel**	10-oz. pkg.	In 1-quart casserole, place 2 tablespoons water.	High (10)	6 to 8
Corn on the Cob	**Fresh**	1 to 5 ears	In 2 or 3-quart oblong glass baking dish, place corn. If corn is in husk, use no water; if corn has been husked, add ¼ cup water.	High (10)	4 to 5 per ear
	Frozen	1 ear	In 2 or 3-quart oblong glass baking dish.	High (10)	6 to 7
		2 to 6 ears		High (10)	3 to 4 per ear
Eggplant	**Fresh**	1 medium (about 1 lb.)	In 2-quart casserole, place 3 tablespoons water. Add peeled and diced eggplant.	High (10)	6 to 8
Okra	**Frozen**	10-oz. pkg.	In 1-quart casserole, place 2 tablespoons water.	High (10)	6 to 8
Parsnips	**Fresh**	1-lb.	In 1½-quart casserole, place ¼ cup water.	High (10)	7 to 10
Peas	**Fresh Shelled**	2-lbs. unshelled	In 1-quart casserole, place ¼ cup water.	High (10)	10 to 13
	Frozen	10-oz. pkg.	In 1-quart casserole, place 2 tablespoons water.	High (10)	6 to 8
Potatoes	**Fresh Whole Sweet or White**	1 (6 to 8-oz. each)	Pierce with cooking fork. Place on paper towel on floor of microwave oven, 1-inch apart in circular arrangement.	High (10)	3 to 5
		4		High (10)	15 to 17
	Fresh Cubed White	4 potatoes (6 to 8-oz. each)	Peel, cut into 1-inch cubes. Place in 2-quart casserole with ½ cup water.	High (10)	12 to 14
Spinach	**Fresh**	10 to 16-oz.	In 2-quart casserole.	High (10)	6 to 8
	Frozen Chopped and Leaf	10-oz. pkg.	In 1-quart casserole, place 3 tablespoons water.	High (10)	6 to 8
Squash	**Fresh Summer and Yellow**	1-lb. sliced	In 1½-quart casserole, place ¼ cup water.	High (10)	7 to 10
	Winter Acorn or Butternut	1 to 2 squash (about 1-lb. each)	Cut in half and remove fibrous membranes. In 8-in. square glass baking dish, place squash cut side down.	High (10)	8 to 11
Succotash	**Frozen**	10-oz. pkg.	In 1-quart casserole, place 2 tablespoons water.	High (10)	8 to 10
Turnips	**Fresh**	1-lb. cubed	In 1½-quart casserole, place 3 tablespoons water.	High (10)	10 to 12
Vegetables, Mixed	**Frozen**	10-oz. pkg.	In 1-quart casserole, place 3 tablespoons water.	High (10)	6 to 8

Pastas, Cereals & Grains

Garden Pasta

3 tablespoons butter
¼ cup onion,
    finely chopped
1 clove garlic, minced
3 tablespoons all-purpose
    flour
½ teaspoon salt
½ teaspoon thyme
2 cups milk
6 slices pasteurized
    American cheese,
    cut into pieces
1 (10 oz.) pkg. frozen
    chopped broccoli,
    thawed & well drained
½ lb. carrots, cut julienne
½ lb. zucchini, sliced
½ lb. fresh mushrooms,
    sliced
1 (8 oz.) pkg. fettuccine,
    cooked and drained

In 3-quart casserole, combine butter, onion and garlic. Microwave at HIGH (10) 2 to 3 minutes until onion is transparent. Stir in flour, salt and thyme. Gradually stir in milk. Microwave at HIGH (10) 5 to 6 minutes, until thickened, stirring every 2 minutes. Blend in cheese, stirring until melted. Set aside.

In 2-quart casserole, combine broccoli, carrots, zucchini and mushrooms. Microwave at HIGH (10) 6 to 9 minutes, until vegetables are tender; stir after 3 minutes. Add vegetables to cheese sauce. Mix well. Serve over fettuccine.

Total Microwave Cooking Time 13 to 18 Minutes
Makes 4 to 6 servings

Deluxe Rice

2 tablespoons butter
1 cup onion, chopped
1½ cups instant rice
½ teaspoon salt
1½ cups water
1 (10 oz.) pkg. frozen
    chopped spinach,
    thawed & drained
1 cup Colby cheese,
    shredded
1 (10 ¾ oz.) can cream of
    mushroom soup
¼ teaspoon hot sauce

In 2-quart casserole, combine butter and onion. Microwave at HIGH (10) 2 to 3 minutes until onion is transparent. Add rice, salt and water. Cover. Microwave at HIGH (10) 3 to 4 minutes. Let stand, covered, 5 minutes. Add spinach, cheese, soup and hot sauce. Mix well. Microwave at MEDIUM (5) 6 to 8 minutes, until heated through; stir after 3 minutes. Let stand, covered, 5 minutes before serving.

TO COOK BY CONVECTION: Place metal accessory rack on floor of oven. Preheat oven to 350°F. Convection Bake 25 to 35 minutes until mixture bubbles around edges.

Total Microwave Cooking Time 11 to 15 Minutes
Total Convection Cooking Time 25 to 35 Minutes
Makes 6 servings

Noodles Alfredo

1 cup grated Parmesan
    cheese
½ cup butter, sliced
½ cup whipping cream
1 tablespoon fresh parsley,
    snipped
3 cups egg noodles, cooked

In 1-quart casserole, combine Parmesan cheese, butter, whipping cream and parsley. Microwave at HIGH (10) 2 to 3 minutes, until butter melts, stirring every minute.

Add noodles. Stir to coat. Microwave at MEDIUM HIGH (7) 2 to 3 minutes until heated through.

Total Microwave Cooking Time 4 to 6 Minutes
Makes 4 to 6 servings

◀ *Garden Pasta*

Pastas, Cereals & Grains

▲ *Pasta Salad*

Pasta Salad

2 cups fresh snow peas
⅓ cup water
2 cups broccoli flowerets
⅓ cup water
2½ cups cherry tomatoes, halved
2 cups fresh mushrooms, sliced
½ cup pitted ripe olives, halved
3 oz. pasta twists, cooked
1 tablespoon grated Parmesan cheese
1 cup hot pepper cheese, cubed

In 2-quart casserole, place snow peas and ⅓ cup water. Cover. Microwave at HIGH (10) 2 minutes. Rinse in cold water immediately. Drain and set aside. Repeat same procedure with broccoli. Drain. Add snow peas, tomatoes, mushrooms, olives, pasta, Parmesan cheese and hot pepper cheese. Toss with pasta salad dressing (see below). Chill several hours before serving.

Total Microwave Cooking Time 4 Minutes
Makes 10 to 12 servings

Pasta Salad Dressing:

½ cup green onions, chopped
⅓ cup red wine vinegar
½ cup vegetable oil
2 tablespoons fresh parsley, snipped
2 cloves garlic, minced
1 teaspoon basil
½ teaspoon salt
½ teaspoon white pepper
½ teaspoon sugar
½ teaspoon oregano
1½ teaspoons Dijon mustard

In a jar, combine green onion, vinegar, vegetable oil, parsley, garlic, basil, salt, pepper, sugar, oregano and mustard. Cover tightly. Shake vigorously until well mixed.

Makes 1¼ cups

Snow Peas and Mushrooms with Wild Rice

1 cup wild rice
6 cups hot tap water
¼ cup carrots, chopped
¼ cup onion, chopped
¼ cup green pepper, chopped
⅓ cup long grain white rice
1 teaspoon marjoram, crushed
2 (10 ½ oz.) cans beef broth
3 tablespoons butter
½ lb. fresh snow peas, sliced diagonally in thirds
½ lb. fresh button mushrooms, stems removed, sliced

In 2-quart casserole, place wild rice and water. Cover. Microwave at HIGH (10) 15 minutes; stir after 7 minutes. Drain. Add carrots, onion, green pepper, white rice, marjoram and beef broth. Cover. Microwave at HIGH (10) 30 to 33 minutes, until all liquid is absorbed, stirring every 10 minutes. In 1-quart casserole, place butter, snow peas and mushrooms. Microwave at HIGH (10) 2 to 3 minutes until tender. Add snow peas and mushrooms to rice. Mix well.

Total Microwave Cooking Time 47 to 51 Minutes
Makes 6 servings

Drain cooked wild rice before adding other ingredients.

Fettuccine with Onions and Bacon

1 tablespoon butter
½ cup onion, chopped
1 clove garlic, minced
3 slices bacon, chopped
½ cup whipping cream
2 tablespoons grated Parmesan cheese
2 tablespoons fresh parsley, snipped
¼ teaspoon salt
½ teaspoon black pepper
1 (8 oz.) pkg. fettuccine, cooked and drained
1 tablespoon grated Parmesan cheese

In 1½-quart casserole, place butter, onion, garlic and bacon. Microwave at HIGH (10) 5 to 6 minutes; stir after 3 minutes. Add cream, Parmesan cheese, parsley, salt, pepper and fettuccine. Mix well. Microwave at HIGH (10) 2 to 3 minutes until heated through. Sprinkle with remaining Parmesan cheese.

Total Microwave Cooking Time 7 to 9 Minutes
Makes 4 servings

Pilaf

3 tablespoons butter
⅓ cup onion, chopped
⅓ cup green pepper, chopped
⅓ cup carrots, shredded
⅓ cup celery, chopped
1 cup water
1 tablespoon instant beef bouillon granules
⅛ teaspoon sage
1 cup instant rice

In 1½-quart casserole, combine butter, onion, green pepper, carrots, celery, water, beef bouillon, sage, pepper and rice. Cover. Microwave at HIGH (10) 8 to 10 minutes; stir after 4 minutes. Let stand, covered, 5 minutes before serving.

Total Microwave Cooking Time 8 to 10 Minutes
Makes 4 to 6 servings

Pastas, Cereals & Grains

Stuff cooked manicotti with cheese filling.

▲ *Cheese Stuffed Manicotti*

Cheese Stuffed Manicotti

1 cup mozzarella cheese, shredded
2 cups Ricotta cheese
½ cup Romano cheese
1 (7 ¾ oz.) can spinach, drained
½ teaspoon garlic powder
½ teaspoon salt
¼ teaspoon pepper
10 manicotti, cooked
1 (15 oz.) can tomato sauce
⅛ teaspoon sweet basil
⅛ teaspoon oregano
1 cup mozzarella cheese, shredded

In medium mixing bowl, combine 1 cup mozzarella, Ricotta, Romano, spinach, garlic powder, salt and pepper. Stuff cooked manicotti with cheese filling. Arrange in 2-quart oblong glass baking dish. Set aside. In 2-cup glass measure, combine tomato sauce, basil and oregano. Pour over top of manicotti. Sprinkle with remaining mozzarella. Cover with wax paper. Microwave at HIGH (10) 15 to 18 minutes, until hot; rotate dish ½ turn after 7 minutes.

TO COOK BY COMBINATION: Place metal accessory rack on floor of oven. Preheat oven to 350°F. Cook on Combination 23 to 28 minutes.

TO COOK BY CONVECTION: Place metal accessory rack on floor of oven. Preheat oven to 350°F. Convection Bake 30 to 35 minutes.

Total Microwave Cooking Time 15 to 18 Minutes
Total Combination Cooking Time 23 to 28 Minutes
Total Convection Cooking Time 30 to 35 Minutes
Makes 5 servings

Hoppin' John

1 lb. bulk pork sausage
½ cup onion, chopped
1 (15 oz.) can black-eyed peas, washed and drained
1 cup instant rice
1 small hot red pepper, crushed
3 cups hot water
½ teaspoon salt
¼ teaspoon pepper

In 3-quart casserole, place sausage and onion. Microwave at HIGH (10) 8 to 10 minutes, until sausage is thoroughly cooked; stir after 4 minutes to break sausage apart. Add black-eyed peas, rice, red pepper, water, salt and pepper. Cover. Microwave at HIGH (10) 10 to 15 minutes until rice is cooked and most of the liquid is absorbed; stir after 5 minutes. Let stand 5 minutes before serving.

Total Microwave Cooking Time 18 to 25 Minutes
Makes 6 to 8 servings

Savory Tomato Rice

4 strips bacon, cooked and crumbled
1 (14 ½ oz.) can tomatoes, undrained, cut up
½ cup long grain white rice
½ cup chili sauce
¼ cup green pepper, finely chopped
2 tablespoons instant minced onion
1 teaspoon brown sugar
½ teaspoon salt
⅛ teaspoon pepper
½ teaspoon Worcestershire sauce
2 cups hot tap water

In 2-quart casserole, place bacon, tomatoes, rice, chili sauce, green pepper, onion, brown sugar, salt, pepper, Worcestershire sauce and water. Mix well. Cover. Microwave at HIGH (10) 20 to 23 minutes, until hot and rice is done, stirring every 8 minutes.

This casserole is very juicy immediately after microwaving. Stir and let stand, uncovered, 5 minutes before serving.

Total Microwave Cooking Time 20 to 23 Minutes
Makes 4 to 6 servings

After microwaving, remove cover and let stand a few minutes before serving.

Cheesy Vegetable Rice

1 ½ cups long grain white rice, cooked
2 cups mozzarella cheese, shredded, divided
2 small zucchini, thinly sliced
1 medium tomato, chopped
1 green onion, chopped
¼ cup celery, chopped
1 teaspoon Italian herb seasoning
1 (8 oz.) container sour cream

In 1 ½-quart casserole, place cooked rice. In layers over rice, place 1 cup cheese, zucchini, tomato, green onion, celery, Italian seasoning and remaining cheese. Cover. Microwave at MEDIUM HIGH (7) 12 to 15 minutes. Spread sour cream evenly over top. Cover. Microwave at MEDIUM HIGH (7) 2 minutes. Let stand 5 minutes, before serving.

Total Microwave Cooking Time 14 to 17 Minutes
Makes 4 servings

Granola

2 ½ cups regular rolled oats
½ cup coconut
½ cup peanuts, coarsely chopped
⅓ cup sunflower seeds
⅓ cup toasted wheat germ
¾ cup honey or molasses
¼ cup vegetable oil
¾ cup mixed dried fruit bits
½ cup pitted dates, chopped
½ cup miniature chocolate chips

In large mixing bowl, combine rolled oats, coconut, peanuts, sunflower seeds and wheat germ. Set aside. In small mixing bowl, combine honey and vegetable oil. Pour over oat mixture, stirring well to coat evenly. Microwave at HIGH (10) 8 to 10 minutes, until mixture is toasted, stirring every 2 minutes. Add dried fruit bits, dates and chocolate chips. Set aside. Line 3-quart oblong glass baking dish with foil. Press the granola mixture into the foil-lined dish. Allow to cool and break into clumps. Store in an air tight container.

Total Microwave Cooking Time 8 to 10 Minutes
Makes 7 cups

After cooling, break into pieces and store in air tight container.

Breads

Braided Egg Bread

2 ¾ cups all-purpose flour
1 (¼ oz.) envelope
   dry yeast
¾ cup water
3 tablespoons butter
2 tablespoons sugar
¼ teaspoon salt
1 egg, beaten

In large mixing bowl, combine 1 cup flour and yeast. Heat and stir water, butter, sugar and salt until warm (120° to 130°). Add to flour mixture along with egg. Beat with electric mixer on low speed for 30 seconds, scraping bowl constantly. Beat on high speed for 3 minutes. Stir in remaining flour to form soft dough. Cover; let rise about 1 hour or until doubled in size. Roll dough out on lightly floured surface into 12x6-inch rectangle. Cut into 3 long strips 12x2-inch each. On lightly greased 14x9-inch cookie sheet, braid the three strips together to make a loaf. Cover; let rise about 1 hour or until doubled in size. Place metal accessory rack on floor of oven. Preheat oven to 375°F. Convection Bake 18 to 20 minutes.

Total Convection Cooking Time 18 to 20 Minutes
Makes 1 French-style loaf

Walnut-Apricot Twist

Dough:
1 (¼ oz.) envelope
   dry yeast
¼ cup granulated sugar
½ cup warm water
¼ cup butter
2 eggs
¼ teaspoon salt
2 cups all-purpose flour

Filling:
¾ cup dried apricots
¼ cup raisins
1 teaspoon grated
   orange rind
1 tablespoon orange juice
¼ cup apricot brandy
2 tablespoons granulated
   sugar
¼ cup walnuts, chopped

Glaze:
¼ cup walnuts, chopped
1 cup powdered sugar
3 teaspoons whipping
   cream
1 teaspoon vanilla

Sprinkle yeast and 1 tablespoon of granulated sugar over warm water in large mixing bowl; stir to dissolve. Let stand until foamy. Mix in butter, eggs, salt and remaining sugar. Add enough flour, 1 cup at a time, to form stiff dough. Cover and chill at least 2 hours.

In 4-cup glass measure, combine apricots, raisins, orange rind, orange juice, apricot brandy and granulated sugar. Microwave at MEDIUM (5) 5 minutes, until mixture thickens and dried fruit softens, stirring every minute. Grease a 10-inch pizza pan. Divide dough into 2 pieces. Roll one piece out on lightly floured surface to form 8-inch circle. Transfer to pan. Spread filling over dough, leaving ½-inch border around edge. Sprinkle nuts over filling. Roll remaining dough into 8-inch circle. Place on top of filling; press edges to seal. Using lightly floured 2-inch cookie cutter, cut all the way through center of dough; do not remove. Using lightly floured pastry wheel and starting ¼-inch from edge of inner circle, cut all the way through dough to outside edge. Repeat 11 times, spacing cuts 1 ½-inches apart at outer edge. Pick up end of 1 dough strip, twist once and replace on baking sheet. Repeat with remaining dough strips. Let dough rise in warm area 35 to 40 minutes or until almost doubled.

Place metal accessory rack on floor of oven. Preheat oven to 350°F. Sprinkle ¼ cup walnuts over dough. Convection Bake 15 to 20 minutes until top is golden brown. In 2-cup glass measure, combine powdered sugar, whipping cream and vanilla; stir until smooth. Drizzle glaze over warm coffee cake. Serve warm.

Total Convection Cooking Time 15 to 20 Minutes
Makes 1 (10-inch) coffee cake

◀ *Braided Egg Bread*

Breads

▲ *Toasted Coconut Pretzels*

Sausage Dressing

1 lb. bulk pork sausage
2 medium onions,
** finely chopped**
1½ cups celery,
** finely chopped**
5 cups cornbread crumbs
6 slices white bread,
** toasted and cubed**
½ teaspoon seasoned salt
⅛ teaspoon coriander
½ teaspoon sweet basil
¼ teaspoon pepper
1 (14½ oz.) can chicken
** broth**
2 eggs, beaten

In 3-quart oblong glass baking dish, combine sausage, onions and celery. Cover with vented plastic wrap. Microwave at HIGH (10) 7 to 8 minutes until sausage is brown and vegetables are tender. Drain and return to casserole. Place metal accessory rack on floor of oven. Preheat oven to 350°F. Add cornbread, bread cubes, seasoned salt, coriander, basil, pepper, chicken broth and eggs to sausage mixture. Stir well. Cook on Combination 28 to 33 minutes until heated through.

Total Combination Cooking Time 28 to 33 Minutes
Makes 8 to 10 servings

Apple Spice Bread

1 cup all-purpose flour
¾ cup sugar
¾ teaspoon cinnamon
½ teaspoon baking soda
¼ teaspoon salt
¼ cup butter, melted
½ cup applesauce
1 egg, beaten
2 tablespoons burgundy
** wine**

Sift flour, sugar, cinnamon, baking soda and salt together. In medium mixing bowl, combine butter, applesauce, egg and burgundy wine. Add flour mixture. Grease a 9-inch round glass baking dish. Fill with batter. Microwave at HIGH (10) 5 to 6 minutes; rotate dish ½ turn after 3 minutes. Cool 15 to 20 minutes.

Total Microwave Cooking Time 5 to 6 Minutes
Makes 8 servings

Toasted Coconut Pretzels

3 cups all-purpose flour
½ cup butter, sliced
1 (¼ oz.) envelope
   dry yeast
¼ cup granulated sugar
¼ cup warm water
1 cup whipping cream
3 egg yolks, beaten
½ teaspoon salt

Topping:
1 egg white
1 cup coconut, shredded
   and toasted
½ cup brown sugar,
   firmly packed

Place flour in large mixing bowl. Cut in butter, with a pastry blender, until mixture resembles coarse meal. Cover and refrigerate. Sprinkle yeast and 1 tablespoon of granulated sugar over warm water in medium mixing bowl; stir to dissolve. Let stand 5 minutes until foamy. Add cream, egg yolks, salt and remaining sugar; stir well. Pour over flour mixture and stir until flour is just moistened. Cover and refrigerate dough at least 12 hours.

Punch dough down. Roll out onto lightly floured surface into 16-inch square. Fold dough over into 3 equal pieces. Starting on the short side, roll dough out into approximately 10x20-inch rectangle. With pizza cutter, cut 10-inch strips approximately ¾-inch wide. Form each strip into a pretzel shape. Brush with egg white. In small mixing bowl, combine coconut and brown sugar; sprinkle on top of each pretzel. Place metal accessory rack on floor of oven. Preheat oven to 350°F. Convection Bake 15 to 17 minutes.

> Total Convection Cooking Time 15 to 17 Minutes
> Makes 20 to 25 pretzels

With pizza cutter, cut 10-inch strips approximately ¾-inch wide.

Form each strip into a pretzel shape. Pinch ends to seal.

Orange-Nut Muffins

2 cups all-purpose flour
⅓ cup sugar
1 teaspoon baking powder
½ teaspoon baking soda
¼ teaspoon salt
1 cup natural nutty cereal
¾ cup raisins
1 cup orange juice
1½ teaspoons grated
   orange rind
⅓ cup vegetable oil

In large mixing bowl, combine flour, sugar, baking powder, baking soda, salt, cereal and raisins. In 2-cup glass measure, blend together orange juice, orange rind and vegetable oil; add to dry ingredients. Blend until moistened. Fill paper-lined, microwave-safe muffin cups ½ full with batter. Microwave at HIGH (10) 2 to 3 minutes. Repeat with remaining batter.

TO COOK BY CONVECTION: Place metal accessory rack on floor of oven. Preheat oven to 375°F. Convection Bake 11 to 13 minutes.

> Total Microwave Cooking Time 2 to 3 Minutes
> Total Convection Cooking Time 11 to 13 Minutes
> Makes 15 to 18 muffins

Zucchini Bread

1¾ cups all-purpose flour
1 teaspoon cinnamon
1 teaspoon baking soda
½ teaspoon salt
1 cup sugar
1 cup zucchini, grated
2 eggs
½ cup vegetable oil
½ cup plain yogurt
1½ teaspoons vanilla
1 cup pecans, chopped

Place metal accessory rack on floor of oven. Preheat oven to 350°F. In small mixing bowl, sift together flour, cinnamon, baking soda and salt. In medium mixing bowl, combine sugar, zucchini, eggs, oil, yogurt and vanilla. Add flour mixture; stir well. Fold in nuts. Pour batter into well-greased and floured 9x5x3-inch loaf pan. Convection Bake 55 to 60 minutes until toothpick inserted in center comes out clean. Remove from pan and let cool on wire rack.

> Total Convection Cooking Time 55 to 60 Minutes
> Makes 12 to 15 servings

Breads

Spicy Corn Muffins

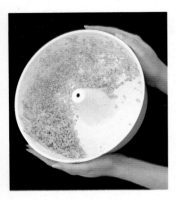
Coat sides and bottom of ring pan with crushed onions.

1 cup self-rising corn meal
½ cup all-purpose flour
1 teaspoon chili powder
½ teaspoon salt
2 tablespoons onion, finely chopped
2 tablespoons honey
2 eggs, beaten
¾ cup buttermilk
2 tablespoons vegetable oil
1 cup French-fried onions, finely crushed

Place metal accessory rack on floor of oven. Preheat oven to 375°F. In medium mixing bowl, sift together corn meal, flour, chili powder and salt. Add onion, honey, eggs, buttermilk and oil. Spoon batter into well-greased muffin pan filling each cup ½ full. Sprinkle French-fried onions over top. Convection Bake 15 to 17 minutes.

Total Convection Cooking Time 15 to 17 Minutes
Makes 10 to 12 servings

To microwave: Place crushed onions in 9-inch buttered microwave baking ring, reserving ¼ cup. Turn to coat sides and bottom. Pour batter into prepared ring. Top with reserved onions. Microwave at MEDIUM (5) 4 to 6 minutes; rotate dish after 3 minutes.

Total Microwave Cooking Time 4 to 6 Minutes
Makes one (9-inch) ring

Dilly-Onion Bread

1 (¼ oz.) envelope dry yeast
¼ cup warm water
1 cup small curd cottage cheese, lukewarm
1 egg, beaten
2 tablespoons sugar
2 tablespoons dill seed
1 teaspoon celery seed
1 tablespoon dried onions
1 teaspoon salt
¼ teaspoon baking soda
2 ¼ cups all-purpose flour
2 tablespoons butter, melted

In large mixing bowl, sprinkle yeast over warm water; stir to dissolve. Mix in cottage cheese, egg, sugar, dill seed, celery seed and dried onions. Sift together salt, baking soda and flour. Add to cottage cheese mixture; stir well. Cover. Let rise, in warm place, 1 hour or until double in size. Stir dough down and pour into well-buttered 8-inch souffle dish. Cover. Let rise about 45 minutes or until almost double in size. Place metal accessory rack on floor of oven. Preheat oven to 350°F. Convection Bake 40 to 45 minutes until browned. Brush with melted butter and cool on wire rack.

Total Convection Cooking Time 40 to 45 Minutes
Makes 6 to 8 servings

Strawberry Bread

1½ cups fresh strawberries, sliced
⅓ cup milk
2 eggs, beaten
½ teaspoon vanilla
½ cup vegetable oil
1½ cups all-purpose flour
½ teaspoon baking soda
½ teaspoon baking powder
¼ teaspoon salt
1½ teaspoons cinnamon
1 cup sugar
½ cup walnuts, chopped

Place metal accessory rack on floor oven. Preheat oven to 350°F. In large mixing bowl, combine strawberries, milk, eggs, vanilla and oil. In medium mixing bowl, sift together flour, baking soda, baking powder, salt, cinnamon and sugar. Add dry ingredients and walnuts to strawberry mixture; stir well. Pour batter into greased and floured 9x5x3-inch loaf pan. Convection Bake 50 to 60 minutes until toothpick inserted in center comes out clean.

Total Convection Cooking Time 50 to 60 Minutes
Makes 1 (9x5-inch) loaf

Raisin Bran Muffins

1 egg, beaten
1 cup buttermilk
1¼ cups all-purpose flour
1 cup bran cereal
½ cup brown sugar, firmly packed
1 teaspoon baking soda
¼ teaspoon salt
¼ cup vegetable oil
½ cup raisins
¼ cup walnuts, chopped

In large mixing bowl, beat egg and buttermilk together. Add flour, cereal, brown sugar, baking soda, salt, oil, raisins and walnuts; stir to blend. Let batter stand 5 minutes. Spoon into paper-lined, microwave-safe muffin pan, filling each cup about half full. Microwave at HIGH (10) 2 to 3 minutes. Repeat with remaining batter.

TO COOK BY CONVECTION: Place metal accessory rack on floor of oven. Preheat oven to 375°F. Spoon batter into paper-lined muffin pan. Convection Bake 10 to 15 minutes.

Total Microwave Cooking Time 2 to 3 Minutes
Total Convection Cooking Time 10 to 15 Minutes
Makes 18 muffins

Surprise Muffins

1 egg, beaten
1 cup milk
¼ cup vegetable oil
2 cups all-purpose flour
¼ cup sugar
2 teaspoons baking powder
½ teaspoon salt
Fruit jelly*

Place metal accessory rack on floor of oven. Preheat oven 375°F. Grease bottom of muffin cups. In medium mixing bowl, combine egg, milk, oil, flour, sugar, baking powder and salt. Fill muffin cups ½ full. Drop teaspoon of jelly in center of batter, add remaining batter to fill cup ⅔ full. Convection Bake 20 to 25 minutes until golden brown.

(*Note: Cream cheese, peanut butter or chocolate chips may be substituted for fruit jelly.)

Total Convection Cooking Time 20 to 25 Minutes
Makes 12 muffins

Drop teaspoon of jelly in center of batter.

Sour Cream Bread

1½ teaspoons baking powder
1 teaspoon baking soda
2 cups all-purpose flour
1 cup sugar
½ cup butter
1 (8 oz.) container sour cream
3 eggs, beaten
2½ teaspoons vanilla
¼ teaspoon almond extract
¾ cup pecans, chopped

Crumb Topping:
⅔ cup all-purpose flour
⅓ cup sugar
⅓ cup butter

Place metal accessory rack on floor of oven. Preheat oven to 350°F. Grease a 9x5x3-inch loaf pan.

In large mixing bowl, combine baking powder, baking soda, flour and sugar. Using a pastry blender, cut in butter until mixture resembles coarse meal. Blend in sour cream, eggs, vanilla and almond extract. Fold in pecans. Pour batter into prepared pan.

In small bowl, combine flour and sugar. Using a pastry blender, cut in butter until mixture resembles coarse crumbs. Sprinkle crumb topping over batter. Convection Bake 50 to 60 minutes until toothpick inserted in center comes out clean.

Total Convection Cooking Time 50 to 60 Minutes
Makes 10 servings

Breads

▲ *Banana Muffins*

Banana Muffins

¾ **cup pecans,**
  coarsely chopped
½ **cup oats, uncooked**
½ **cup corn flakes**
1½ **cups all-purpose flour**
1½ **teaspoons baking**
  powder
1 **teaspoon baking soda**
¼ **teaspoon salt**
2 **large ripe bananas,**
  mashed
½ **cup milk**
½ **cup honey**
2 **tablespoons butter,**
  melted
1 **egg**

Place metal accessory rack on floor of oven. Preheat oven to 375°F. In large mixing bowl, combine pecans, oats, corn flakes, flour, baking powder, baking soda and salt. In medium mixing bowl, beat together bananas, milk, honey, butter and egg. Add banana mixture to dry ingredients; stir until moistened. Spoon batter into paper-lined muffin pans. Convection Bake 15 to 19 minutes until golden brown.

Total Convection Cooking Time 15 to 19 Minutes
Makes 12 muffins

Buttery Almond Crown

3 cups all-purpose flour
1¼ cups butter, sliced
2 (¼ oz.) envelopes
   dry yeast
¼ cup sugar
¼ cup warm water
½ cup evaporated milk
2 eggs, beaten
½ teaspoon salt
½ teaspoon butter
   flavoring

Filling:
½ cup butter
½ cup sugar
½ cup almond paste
½ teaspoon almond
   extract
¼ cup slivered almonds,
   toasted

Place flour in large mixing bowl. Using a pastry blender, cut in butter until mixture resembles coarse meal. In medium mixing bowl, sprinkle yeast and 1 tablespoon of sugar over warm water; stir to dissolve. Let stand 5 minutes until foamy. Add milk, eggs, salt, butter flavoring and remaining sugar. Pour over flour mixture and stir until flour is just moistened. Cover and refrigerate at least 5 hours or overnight. In medium mixing bowl, cream ½ cup butter, sugar, almond paste and almond extract with an electric mixer; set aside. Butter 12-cup bundt pan and sprinkle bottom with almonds. Set aside. Roll chilled dough out on waxed paper into 27x9-inch rectangle. Spread filling on dough. Cut dough into thirds. Roll each third in jelly roll fashion and cut crosswise into three pieces. Arrange slices cut side down in bottom of Bundt pan. Let rise in warm place about 1½ hours or until almost double in size. Place metal accessory rack on floor of oven. Preheat oven to 350°F. Convection Bake 35 to 40 minutes until top is golden brown. Let cool on rack.

Total Convection Cooking Time 35 to 40 Minutes
Makes 12 servings

Arrange dough slices cut side down in bottom of pan. Space evenly.

Oatmeal-Orange Coffee Cake

1½ cups all-purpose flour
1 cup oats, uncooked
⅓ cup brown sugar,
   firmly packed
1 tablespoon baking
   powder
½ teaspoon baking soda
2 ripe bananas, mashed
½ cup orange juice
⅓ cup butter, melted
1 egg, beaten
¼ teaspoon orange rind,
   grated
½ teaspoon vanilla
½ cup powdered sugar
1 tablespoon orange juice
¼ teaspoon orange rind,
   grated

Place metal accessory rack on floor of oven. Preheat oven to 350°F. In large mixing bowl, combine flour, oats, brown sugar, baking powder and baking soda. Combine bananas, orange juice, butter, egg, orange rind and vanilla. Add to flour mixture. Mix until moistened. Grease the bottom only of 9-inch round springform pan. Pour batter into pan. Convection Bake 22 to 25 minutes until golden brown. Cool 10 minutes on wire rack; remove from pan.

In small mixing bowl, combine powdered sugar, orange juice and orange rind. Drizzle evenly over cake while still warm.

Total Convection Cooking Time 22 to 25 Minutes
Makes 1 (9-inch) coffee cake

Breads

Cinnamon Bread ▲

Old Fashioned Biscuits

2 cups all-purpose flour
¼ cup sugar
1 tablespoon baking
   powder
¼ teaspoon salt
¼ cup butter
1 cup whipping cream

Place metal accessory rack on floor of oven. Preheat oven to 400°F. In large mixing bowl, combine flour, sugar, baking powder and salt. Using a pastry blender, cut in butter until mixture resembles coarse meal. Add cream. Stir until mixture forms stiff dough. Turn dough onto lightly floured surface. Knead to mix thoroughly. Roll out dough to ½-inch thickness. Using a floured 2½-inch biscuit cutter, cut out biscuits. Place on ungreased cookie sheet, 1-inch apart. Convection Bake 10 to 12 minutes until biscuits are golden brown.

Total Convection Cooking Time 10 to 12 Minutes
Makes about 1 dozen

Banana Bread

¾ cup sugar
½ cup butter
2 ripe bananas, mashed
2 teaspoons lemon juice
⅓ cup milk
2 eggs, beaten
1½ cups all-purpose flour
1 teaspoon baking soda
½ teaspoon baking
   powder
½ cup walnuts, chopped

Place metal accessory rack on floor of oven. Preheat oven to 350°F. Grease a 9x5x3-inch loaf pan. In large mixing bowl, cream sugar and butter with an electric mixer. Mix in mashed bananas and lemon juice; add milk and eggs. Sift in flour, baking soda and baking powder. Blend well. Stir in nuts. Pour into prepared pan. Convection Bake 45 to 55 minutes.

Total Convection Cooking Time 45 to 55 Minutes
Makes 1 (9-inch) loaf

Cinnamon Bread

⅓ cup sugar
1 tablespoon salt
½ cup shortening
1 cup milk, scalded
½ cup cold water
2 (¼ oz.) envelopes
　dry yeast
¼ cup warm water
1 egg, beaten
5 ½ to 6 cups all-purpose
　flour
1 tablespoon butter,
　softened
¼ cup sugar
2 teaspoons cinnamon

In large mixing bowl, combine sugar, salt, shortening and hot milk; stir until shortening melts. Add water. In 2-cup glass measure, dissolve yeast and warm water; add to milk mixture. Add egg; stir well. Add enough flour to form soft dough. Knead on floured surface 3 minutes until smooth. Place in large well-greased mixing bowl greased-side up. Let rise 1 hour until doubled in size, punch down.

In small mixing bowl, combine sugar and cinnamon. On lightly floured surface, roll dough to 12x9-inch rectangle. Spread with butter and sugar-cinnamon mixture. Starting from long side, roll in jelly roll fashion. Place on greased cookie sheet and let rise until doubled in size. Place metal accessory rack on floor of oven. Preheat oven to 350°F. Convection Bake 25 to 30 minutes until golden brown.

Total Convection Cooking Time 25 to 30 Minutes
Makes 1 French-style loaf

Evenly sprinkle sugar-cinnamon mixture over dough.

Starting from long side, roll in jelly roll fashion.

Mushroom Stuffing

½ lb. fresh mushrooms,
　sliced
½ cup onion, chopped
½ cup celery, chopped
½ cup butter
1 egg, beaten
1 (8 oz.) pkg. seasoned
　stuffing mix
1 cup hot water
2 teaspoons instant
　chicken bouillon
　granules
1 teaspoon ground sage
½ teaspoon pepper

In 2-quart casserole, combine mushrooms, onion, celery and butter. Microwave at HIGH (10) 5 to 8 minutes until vegetables are tender. Add egg, stuffing mix, water, bouillon, ground sage and pepper. Microwave at HIGH (10) 4 to 6 minutes, until heated through; stir after 2 minutes.

TO COOK BY CONVECTION: Place metal accessory rack on floor of oven. Preheat oven to 350°F. Convection Bake 30 to 35 minutes.

Total Microwave Cooking Time 9 to 14 Minutes
Total Convection Cooking Time 30 to 35 Minutes
Makes 6 to 8 servings

Buttery Batter Bread

1 cup warm milk
　(110° to 115°)
¾ cup butter, melted
¼ cup sugar
1 ½ teaspoons salt
1 (¼ oz.) pkg. dry yeast
4 cups all-purpose flour
4 eggs, slightly beaten

In large mixing bowl, combine milk, butter, sugar and salt. Add yeast; stir to dissolve.

Add 2 cups flour and eggs. Beat with an electric mixer at medium speed 2 minutes until smooth. Stir in remaining 2 cups flour. Let rise 1 hour. Stir down and pour into well-greased, 10-inch tube pan. Cover; let rise about 45 minutes or until doubled in size. Place metal accessory rack on floor of oven. Preheat oven to 350°F. Convection Bake 30 to 35 minutes.

Total Convection Cooking Time 30 to 35 Minutes
Makes 1 loaf

Desserts

Fruit Tart

Pastry Cream:
2 cups milk
½ cup sugar
4 tablespoons all-purpose
    flour
2 egg yolks, beaten
1 tablespoon butter
2 teaspoons vanilla

Crust:
1⅓ cups all-purpose flour
2 tablespoons sugar
½ teaspoon salt
7 tablespoons butter
1 egg yolk, beaten
2 to 3 tablespoons
    ice water

Fruit topping:
4 kiwi fruits, peeled and
    sliced
1 pint raspberries
1 pint strawberries, halved
    lengthwise
1 (11 oz.) can Mandarin
    oranges, drained
½ cup apricot preserves,
    warmed

Place milk in medium mixing bowl and Microwave at MEDIUM HIGH (7) 8 minutes until milk is scalded. Add sugar and flour. Microwave at HIGH (10) 2 to 3 minutes, stirring every 30 seconds. Add egg yolks, butter and vanilla. Microwave at HIGH (10) 2 to 3 minutes, stirring every 30 seconds. Cover with plastic wrap and refrigerate until chilled.

In medium mixing bowl, combine flour, sugar and salt. Cut in butter with pastry blender until mixture resembles coarse meal. Add egg yolk and water, tossing lightly with fork until mixture is evenly moistened and binds together. Form dough into a ball and flatten slightly. Wrap with plastic wrap and refrigerate 30 minutes.

Place metal accessory rack on floor of oven. Preheat oven to 400°F. Roll out dough on lightly floured surface to about ⅛-inch thickness. Line bottom and sides of 9-inch fluted tart pan. Prick the bottom. Line dough with aluminum foil and fill with pie weights or dried beans. Convection Bake 8 minutes. Remove aluminum foil and weights; lower oven temperature to 375°F. and bake for 7 to 9 minutes until golden brown. Cool on wire rack. Spread pastry cream in tart shell. Arrange fruit over cream. Brush lightly with apricot preserves.

Total Microwave Cooking Time 12 to 14 Minutes
Total Convection Cooking Time 15 to 17 Minutes
Makes 8 to 10 servings

Pear and Spice Cake

2 cups all-purpose flour
1 teaspoon cinnamon
1 teaspoon baking soda
½ teaspoon allspice
¼ teaspoon salt
1½ cups brown sugar,
    firmly packed
½ cup vegetable oil
3 eggs
¼ cup granulated sugar
¼ cup water
1 teaspoon vanilla
1 (16 oz.) can pears,
    drained, cut into
    ¼-inch pieces
½ cup pecans, chopped

Place metal accessory rack on floor of oven. Preheat oven to 350°F. Grease and flour a 13x9x2-inch pan.

In medium mixing bowl, sift together flour, cinnamon, baking soda, allspice and salt. In large mixing bowl, combine brown sugar, oil, eggs, granulated sugar, water and vanilla. Beat with an electric mixer until smooth. Add dry ingredients. Blend well. Stir in pears and pecans. Pour batter into prepared pan. Convection Bake 40 to 45 minutes until top is brown and toothpick inserted in center comes out clean.

Total Convection Cooking Time 40 to 45 Minutes
Makes 12 servings

Desserts

▲ *Chocolate Cheesecake*

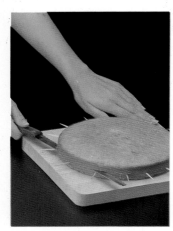

Use toothpicks as a guide to slice cake evenly.

Boston Cream Pie

1 (8-inch) round yellow layer cake

Filling:
½ cup sugar
2 tablespoons cornstarch
1⅔ cups milk
1 egg, beaten
¾ teaspoon vanilla
¼ teaspoon butter flavoring
1 cup whipping cream, whipped

Glaze:
2 (1 oz.) squares unsweetened chocolate
2 tablespoons butter
1¼ cups powdered sugar, sifted
1¼ teaspoons vanilla
3 to 4 tablespoons hot water

Prepare layer cake according to Convection Baking Chart, page 134. Cool completely and cut into 2 thin layers.

In 2-quart casserole, combine sugar, cornstarch and milk. Stir well with a wire whisk. Microwave at HIGH (10) 5 to 7 minutes, until thickened, stirring every 2 minutes. Add egg, vanilla and butter flavoring. Cool completely. Fold whipped cream into thickened mixture. Spread filling between cake layers.

In 4-cup glass measure, combine chocolate and butter. Microwave at HIGH (10) 1 to 2 minutes until chocolate is melted. Add powdered sugar and vanilla. Blend in hot water 1 tablespoon at a time until glaze is desired consistency. Spread over top and sides of cake.

Total Microwave Cooking Time 6 to 9 Minutes
Makes 6 to 8 servings

Chocolate Cheesecake

1 ¼ cups chocolate wafer crumbs
¼ cup butter, melted
8 (1 oz.) squares semisweet chocolate
3 (8 oz.) pkgs. cream cheese, softened
1 cup sugar
3 eggs
2 tablespoons Kahlua
1 teaspoon vanilla
1 ½ cups sour cream
½ cup semisweet chocolate chips

In small mixing bowl, combine chocolate wafer crumbs and butter; stir well. Press crumb mixture into bottom and 1-inch up sides of 9-inch springform pan. Chill. In 4-cup glass measure, place chocolate squares. Microwave at HIGH (10) 2 to 3 minutes until melted. Place metal accessory rack on floor of oven. Preheat oven to 325°F. In medium mixing bowl, beat together cream cheese and sugar with an electric mixer until light and fluffy. Beat in eggs, melted chocolate, Kahlua and vanilla until smooth. Fold in sour cream. Pour mixture into crumb crust. Convection Bake 1 hour. Turn oven off and let cheesecake stand in oven 30 minutes. Remove and cool on wire rack. Cover and chill at least 8 hours. Garnish with chocolate leaves.

To make chocolate leaves: Microwave chocolate chips at HIGH (10) ½ to 1 minute until melted. Brush chocolate on leaves. Chill until set. Carefully peel leaf away from chocolate.

Total Convection Cooking Time 1 Hour
Makes one 9-inch cheesecake

Melt chocolate chips and gently brush on leaves.

Bananas Foster

3 medium bananas, peeled
Lemon juice
½ cup pecans, halved
3 tablespoons butter
½ cup brown sugar, firmly packed
½ teaspoon vanilla
2 tablespoons orange or apple juice
2 tablespoons light rum (optional)
Vanilla ice cream

In 9-inch pie plate, slice bananas in half crosswise and then lengthwise. Brush with lemon juice and sprinkle with pecans. In 2-cup glass measure, combine butter, brown sugar, vanilla and orange or apple juice. Microwave at HIGH (10) 1 minute. Pour sauce over bananas. Microwave at HIGH (10) 2 to 3 minutes until bananas are tender. Add rum, if desired. Serve warm with ice cream.

Total Microwave Cooking Time 3 to 4 Minutes
Makes 4 servings

Chill until set and peel chocolate away from leaf.

Mint Chocolate Chip Pie

1 cup sugar
½ cup butter, melted
½ cup all-purpose flour
2 large eggs
1 teaspoon peppermint extract
1 cup (6 oz.) semisweet chocolate chips
1 cup pecans, chopped
1 (9-inch) pie shell

Place metal accessory rack on floor of oven. Preheat oven to 350°F. In large mixing bowl, combine sugar, butter, flour, eggs, peppermint extract, chocolate chips and pecans. Pour mixture into pie shell. Convection Bake 45 to 50 minutes until filling is golden brown.

Total Convection Cooking Time 45 to 50 Minutes
Makes 8 servings

Desserts

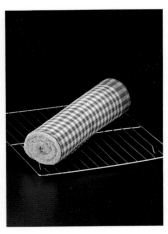

After baking, place cake on towel and roll together.

When cooled, unroll cake and spread with filling.

Pecan Cream Roll

4 eggs, separated
1½ teaspoons vanilla
Dash salt
½ cup granulated sugar
¼ cup all-purpose flour, sifted
¾ cup pecans, finely chopped
Powdered sugar

Filling:
2 cups whipping cream
½ cup granulated sugar

Place metal accessory rack on floor of oven. Preheat oven to 350°F. In medium mixing bowl, beat egg whites, vanilla and salt with an electric mixer until soft peaks form. Gradually add granulated sugar, beating until stiff peaks form. Fold beaten egg yolks into whites. Carefully fold in flour and pecans. Spread batter evenly into greased and floured 15x10x1-inch jelly roll pan. Convection Bake 12 to 14 minutes. Immediately loosen sides and turn out onto towel sprinkled with powdered sugar. Starting at narrow end, roll cake and towel together; cool on wire rack. In medium mixing bowl, beat whipping cream until soft peaks form. Add granulated sugar and continue beating until firm. Unroll cake and spread with ¾ of filling. Roll cake and use remaining filling to decorate top; chill.

Total Convection Cooking Time 12 to 14 Minutes
Makes 8 servings

Caramel Bundt Cake

1 (18 oz.) box yellow cake mix
⅓ cup creamy peanut butter
4 eggs
¾ cup water
¼ teaspoon vanilla
⅓ cup vegetable oil
1 cup unsalted peanuts, chopped
1 cup (6 oz.) semisweet chocolate chips

Caramel Glaze:
2 tablespoons butter, melted
¾ cup brown sugar, firmly packed
1 teaspoon cornstarch
¼ cup whipping cream
½ teaspoon vanilla

Place metal accessory rack on floor of oven. Preheat oven to 350°F. In large mixing bowl, combine cake mix, peanut butter, eggs, water, vanilla and oil. Beat on medium speed for 3 minutes with an electric mixer. Grease and flour a 12-cup bundt pan. Pour in one-third of the cake batter, sprinkle one-third cup peanuts and one-third cup chocolate chips over batter. Repeat with remaining batter, peanuts and chocolate chips. Convection Bake 35 to 40 minutes. Top with Caramel Glaze.

Total Convection Cooking Time 35 to 40 Minutes
Makes 8 to 10 servings

In 4-cup glass measure, combine butter, brown sugar and cornstarch. Mix until smooth. Gradually add whipping cream, stirring to blend. Microwave at HIGH (10) 2 to 3 minutes until thickened. Stir in vanilla.

Total Microwave Cooking Time 2 to 3 Minutes
Makes 1¼ cups

Pecan Pie

3 tablespoons butter, melted
3 eggs, beaten
1 cup light corn syrup
1 cup sugar
1¼ teaspoons vanilla
1 cup pecan pieces
1 (9-inch) pie shell

Place metal accessory rack on floor of oven. Preheat oven to 350°F. In large mixing bowl, combine butter, eggs, corn syrup, sugar and vanilla. Blend well. Stir in pecan pieces. Pour filling into pie shell. Convection Bake 45 to 50 minutes until pie is set in the center. Cool.

Total Convection Cooking Time 45 to 50 Minutes
Makes 1 (9-inch) pie

▲ *Apple Pie*

Apple Pie

2 lbs. baking apples,
   peeled and sliced
1 tablespoon lemon juice
¾ cup sugar
2 tablespoons all-purpose
   flour
1¼ teaspoons cinnamon
⅛ teaspoon nutmeg
⅛ teaspoon salt
¼ teaspoon almond
   extract
½ cup raisins
Butter
1 (2-crust 9-inch) pastry

Place metal accessory rack on floor of oven. Preheat oven to 400°F. In large mixing bowl, toss sliced apples with lemon juice. In small mixing bowl, combine sugar, flour, cinnamon, nutmeg and salt; add to apples and toss until well coated. Add almond extract and raisins. Pour apple mixture into pastry-lined pie plate. Dot with butter. Top with remaining pastry and flute the edges. Slit top of pastry to vent. Convection Bake 55 to 60 minutes until crust is lightly browned.

**Total Convection Cooking Time 55 to 60 Minutes
Makes 8 servings**

Cream Puffs

½ cup water
¼ cup butter
½ cup all-purpose flour
⅛ teaspoon salt
2 eggs
Prepared Pastry Cream,
   page 117

In 2-quart casserole, combine water and butter. Microwave at HIGH (10) 2 to 3 minutes until mixture boils. Beat in flour and salt until dough forms a ball and leaves the sides of the bowl. Microwave at HIGH (10) 1 minute. Place metal accessory rack on floor of oven. Preheat oven to 400°F. Add eggs to flour mixture one at a time, beating with an electric mixer until smooth and glossy. Drop batter in 6 mounds onto ungreased cookie sheet. Convection Bake 20 to 25 minutes. Cut slit in side of each puff to allow steam to escape. Bake 5 minutes longer. Remove from cookie sheet and cool on metal cake rack. To fill puffs, slice off tops. Spoon pastry cream into center; replace tops. Serve immediately.

To fill, slice off tops and spoon filling into center.

**Total Convection Cooking Time 25 to 30 Minutes
Makes 6 servings**

Desserts

▲ *Peach Torte*

Peach Torte

3 tablespoons butter
½ cup brown sugar,
  firmly packed
1 egg
1 teaspoon vanilla
¾ cup all-purpose flour
¼ teaspoon baking soda
¼ teaspoon salt
½ cup milk
½ cup graham cracker
  crumbs
⅓ cup pecans, chopped
1 cup fresh peaches,
  peeled and sliced
Lemon juice
1 cup whipping cream

Place metal accessory rack on floor of oven. Preheat oven to 325°F. Grease bottom of 8-inch round cake pan and line with wax paper. In medium mixing bowl, cream butter and brown sugar with an electric mixer until light and fluffy. Add egg and vanilla. Stir well to blend. Gradually blend in flour, baking soda, salt and milk. Fold in cracker crumbs and pecans. Spread batter into pan. Convection Bake 25 to 30 minutes. Cool on wire rack for 5 minutes. Invert onto wire rack and remove wax paper. Cool 10 minutes. Split cake into 2 layers. Brush fresh peaches with lemon juice.

In small mixing bowl, beat whipping cream with an electric mixer until soft peaks form. Spread one-half of whipped cream on bottom layer and top with peach slices, reserving enough peach slices to garnish the top. Add remaining cake layer. Spread remaining whipping cream over top of cake and garnish with reserved peaches. Chill 2 hours.

Total Convection Cooking Time 25 to 30 Minutes
Makes 6 to 8 servings

Sour Cream Cake

1 cup butter
1½ cups sugar
2 eggs
1 cup sour cream
1 teaspoon vanilla
2 cups all-purpose flour
1 teaspoon baking powder
¼ teaspoon salt

Place metal accessory rack on floor of oven. Preheat oven to 300°F. In medium mixing bowl, cream butter and sugar with an electric mixer until light and fluffy. Beat in eggs, sour cream and vanilla. Gradually add flour, baking powder and salt. Place batter into well-greased and floured 9-inch bundt pan. Convection Bake 1 hour to 1 hour 10 minutes, until toothpick inserted in center comes out clean. Cool on wire rack after removing from pan.

Total Convection Cooking Time 1 Hour to 1 Hour 10 Minutes
Makes about 12 servings

Banana Walnut Tart

3 cups milk
4 egg yolks, beaten
⅔ cup sugar
¼ cup cornstarch
1 (8 oz.) pkg. cream
   cheese, cut into chunks
2 teaspoons vanilla
1 teaspoon butter flavoring
1 cup all-purpose flour
⅓ cup walnuts,
   finely chopped
½ cup butter
2 tablespoons sugar
2 large bananas,
   peeled and sliced
¾ cup coconut, shredded
   and toasted

In 2-quart casserole, combine milk, egg yolks, sugar and cornstarch. Microwave at MEDIUM HIGH (7) 8 to 10 minutes, stirring every 2 minutes. Add cream cheese; stir with a wire whisk until melted. Stir in vanilla and butter flavoring. Microwave at MEDIUM HIGH (7) 6 to 8 minutes, until mixture thickens, stirring every 2 minutes. Cover and refrigerate. Place metal accessory rack on floor of oven. Preheat oven to 325°F. In medium mixing bowl, combine flour, walnuts, butter and sugar. Blend with an electric mixer on low speed to form a soft dough. Press into bottom of 9-inch round tart pan. Convection Bake 20 to 25 minutes until golden brown. Let cool for 10 minutes. Layer bananas onto the crust and top with custard filling. Sprinkle with coconut. Refrigerate for one hour before serving.

Total Microwave Cooking Time 14 to 18 Minutes
Total Convection Cooking Time 20 to 25 Minutes
Makes 8 servings

Lemon Cooler Cookies

1 cup butter
½ cup granulated sugar
1 tablespoon fresh
   lemon rind, grated
1 egg yolk
½ teaspoon lemon extract
½ teaspoon vanilla
2¼ cups all-purpose flour
Granulated sugar
Powdered sugar

Place metal accessory rack on floor of oven. Preheat oven to 350°F. In medium mixing bowl, cream butter and granulated sugar with an electric mixer until light and fluffy. Beat in lemon rind, egg yolk, lemon extract and vanilla. Gradually add flour and beat until blended. Roll 1 tablespoon of dough to form ball. Place on ungreased cookie sheet. Dip bottom of 2½-inch round glass into sugar. Using bottom of glass, flatten to ¼-inch thickness. Convection Bake 9 to 12 minutes until cookie edges begin to brown. Let cool on wire rack. Sift powdered sugar over top.

Total Convection Cooking Time 9 to 12 Minutes
Makes about 3½ dozen cookies

Use bottom of glass dipped in sugar to flatten cookies.

Desserts

▲ *Three Layer Brownies, Peanutty Chocolate Chip Cookies and Lemon Squares*

Lemon Squares

1 cup all-purpose flour
¼ cup powdered sugar
Dash salt
½ cup butter
2 eggs
1 cup granulated sugar
2 tablespoons all-purpose
   flour
½ teaspoon baking
   powder
1 tablespoon fresh
   lemon rind, grated
2 tablespoons lemon juice

Place metal accessory rack on floor of oven. Preheat oven to 350°F. In small mixing bowl, combine 1 cup flour, powdered sugar and salt. Cut in butter until mixture is the size of peas. Grease the bottom of an 8-inch square baking dish. Press mixture evenly into baking dish. Bake for 15 to 20 minutes until set.

In medium mixing bowl, blend eggs, granulated sugar, 2 tablespoons flour, baking powder, lemon rind and lemon juice. Pour mixture over crust. Return to oven. Convection Bake 15 to 20 minutes.

**Total Convection Cooking Time 30 to 40 Minutes
Makes 24 bars**

Peanutty Chocolate Chip Cookies

1 cup butter, softened
1 cup brown sugar,
   firmly packed
½ cup granulated sugar
1⅓ cups (12 oz. jar)
   chunky peanut butter
1 egg
1½ teaspoons vanilla
1½ teaspoons butter
   flavoring
Dash salt
1½ cups all-purpose flour
2 cups (12 oz.) semisweet
   chocolate chips
1 cup dry roasted peanuts,
   chopped

Place metal accessory rack on floor of oven. Preheat oven to 350°F. Lightly grease cookie sheet. In medium mixing bowl, cream butter, brown sugar and granulated sugar with an electric mixer until fluffy. Add peanut butter, egg, vanilla, butter flavoring and salt and continue to mix with an electric mixer until well blended. Stir in flour, chocolate chips and peanuts. For each cookie, place 1 tablespoon of dough onto greased cookie sheet, then flatten to ¼-inch thickness. Space cookies about ½-inch apart. Convection Bake 13 to 15 minutes until golden brown. Let stand 3 minutes, then remove to wire rack to cool.

**Total Convection Cooking Time 13 to 15 Minutes
Makes about 3 dozen cookies**

Three Layer Brownies

¾ cup quick-cooking oats
⅓ cup all-purpose flour
⅓ cup light brown sugar,
  firmly packed
¼ teaspoon baking soda
¼ cup butter, melted
1 (1 oz.) square
  unsweetened chocolate
4 tablespoons butter
⅓ cup granulated sugar
2 tablespoons water
1 egg, beaten
¾ teaspoon vanilla
½ cup all-purpose flour
¼ teaspoon baking powder
½ cup pecans, chopped

Frosting:
1 (1 oz.) square
  unsweetened chocolate
1 tablespoon butter
1 cup powdered sugar,
  sifted
½ teaspoon almond extract
2 tablespoons hot water

In small mixing bowl, combine oats, ⅓ cup flour, brown sugar, baking soda and ¼ cup butter. Press mixture into 8-inch square baking dish. Microwave at MEDIUM (5) 3 to 5 minutes, until surface appears dry; turn dish ¼ turn after 2 minutes. Let cool on wire rack 10 minutes. In 2-quart casserole, combine chocolate and 4 tablespoons butter. Microwave at HIGH (10) 2 to 3 minutes until melted. Add granulated sugar, water, egg, vanilla, flour, baking powder and pecans. Mix well. Spread mixture evenly over oat mixture. Microwave at MEDIUM (5) 5 to 7 minutes; turn dish ¼ turn after 3 minutes. Let cool. Frost with Chocolate Frosting.

Chocolate Frosting: In 1-quart casserole, combine chocolate and butter. Microwave at HIGH (10) 2 to 3 minutes until melted. Add powdered sugar and almond extract. Add hot water, 1 tablespoon at a time, until frosting is spreadable.

Total Microwave Cooking Time 12 to 18 Minutes
Makes about 2 dozen bars

Basic Brownies

2 eggs
1 cup sugar
½ teaspoon salt
1 teaspoon vanilla
½ cup butter, melted
¾ cup all-purpose flour
½ cup cocoa
1 cup chopped nuts

In small bowl at medium speed of electric mixer, beat together eggs, sugar, salt and vanilla 1 minute or until light. Add melted butter. Continue beating until thoroughly blended. Mix in flour and cocoa at low speed. Stir in nuts. Spread evenly in greased 8-inch square baking dish. Microwave at HIGH (10) 6 to 7 minutes; rotate dish ½ turn after 3 minutes. When done, top looks dry and will spring back when lightly touched. Cut when cool.

Total Microwave Cooking Time 6 to 7 Minutes
Makes about 16 brownie squares

Peanut Brittle

1 cup sugar
½ cup light corn syrup
1 cup dry-roasted peanuts
1 teaspoon butter
1 teaspoon vanilla
1 teaspoon baking soda

In 1½-quart casserole, combine sugar and syrup. Microwave at HIGH (10) 3 minutes. Add peanuts. Microwave at HIGH (10) 5 to 7 minutes, until peanuts are light brown, stirring every 2 minutes. Add butter and vanilla; stir well. Add baking soda and gently stir until light and foamy. Pour mixture onto lightly greased cookie sheet. Let cool 30 minutes to 1 hour. When cool, break into small pieces.

Total Microwave Cooking Time 8 to 10 Minutes
Makes about 1 pound

Desserts

▲ *Fruit-Filled Pineapple*

Fruit-Filled Pineapple

1 medium-size fresh
   pineapple
1 (11 oz.) can Mandarin
   oranges, drained
1 cup shredded coconut
½ cup maraschino
   cherries, drained and
   cut in half
½ cup orange marmalade
½ cup toasted, sliced
   almonds
2 tablespoons light rum

Cut leafy crown off pineapple; reserve for garnish, if desired. Cut pineapple in half lengthwise. Scoop out fruit, leaving 1/4-inch shell. Remove woody core from fruit and discard. Cut remaining fruit into chunks.

Combine pineapple chunks, oranges, coconut, cherries, marmalade, almonds, and rum; toss gently. Place shells in 3-quart oblong glass baking dish. Divide fruit mixture evenly between shells. Cover with wax paper. Microwave at High (10) 7 to 9 minutes or until heated through.

Total Microwave Cooking Time 7 to 9 Minutes
Makes 6 servings

Turtle Cake

25 caramel candies,
  unwrapped
¼ cup evaporated milk
¼ cup butter, melted
1 (9 oz.) box chocolate
  cake mix
2 tablespoons evaporated
  milk
½ cup semisweet
  chocolate chips
½ cup pecans, chopped

In medium mixing bowl, combine caramels and ¼ cup evaporated milk. Microwave at HIGH (10) 2 to 3 minutes, stirring every 30 seconds. In large mixing bowl, combine butter, cake mix and 2 tablespoons evaporated milk. Press one-half of cake mixture into lightly greased 8-inch square baking dish. Microwave at HIGH (10) 3 minutes. Sprinkle chocolate chips and pecans on top. Spread caramel mixture over chocolate chips and pecans. Crumble remaining cake mix over caramel mixture. Microwave at HIGH (10) 4 to 5 minutes. Cool completely.

Total Microwave Cooking Time 9 to 11 Minutes
Makes 10 to 12 servings

To prepare caramel mixture, combine caramels and evaporated milk then microwave.

Toffee Cake

2 cups all-purpose flour
1½ cups light brown sugar,
  firmly packed
Dash salt
½ cup butter
1 cup buttermilk
1 egg, beaten
1 teaspoon vanilla
1 teaspoon baking soda
5 (1.2 oz.) pkgs. chocolate
  covered English toffee,
  coarsely chopped
⅓ cup walnuts, chopped

Place metal accessory rack on floor of oven. Preheat oven to 350°F. Grease a 13x9x2-inch cake pan. In large mixing bowl, combine flour, brown sugar and salt. With a pastry blender, cut in butter until mixture resembles coarse meal. Remove 1 cup flour mixture and place in medium mixing bowl; set aside. Add buttermilk, egg, vanilla and baking soda. Mix until well blended. Pour batter evenly into prepared pan. In medium mixing bowl, mix reserved flour mixture, toffee and walnuts. Sprinkle toffee mixture over batter. Convection Bake 35 to 45 minutes until toothpick inserted in center comes out clean.

Total Convection Cooking Time 35 to 45 Minutes
Makes 12 servings

Chocolate Chip Bars

½ cup butter, melted
¾ cup light brown sugar,
  firmly packed
2 eggs, beaten
¾ teaspoon vanilla
¼ teaspoon almond
  extract
¾ cup walnuts, chopped
1 cup (6 oz.) semisweet
  chocolate chips
½ cup all-purpose flour
1 teaspoon baking powder
Powdered sugar

In medium mixing bowl, combine butter, brown sugar, eggs, vanilla and almond extract. Stir until blended. Add walnuts, chocolate chips, flour and baking powder. Mix well. Pour batter into 8-inch square glass baking dish. Microwave at HIGH (10) 6 to 8 minutes until toothpick inserted in center comes out clean; rotate dish ¼ turn after 3 minutes. Sprinkle with powdered sugar.

Total Microwave Cooking Time 6 to 8 Minutes
Makes 24 bars

Microwaving Guide

1. Refer to the chart below when microwaving raw or uncooked foods.
2. Since microwaving does not brown food as in conventional cooking, you may prefer to convection bake or combination cook foods such as meats and baked goods.
3. Always cook in microwave-safe plastic, glass or oven-safe plastic containers. *DO NOT USE METAL CONTAINERS.* Paper, under some circumstances, can be used. When covering with plastic wrap, turn one corner back to vent.
4. When using microwave plastic containers be sure oven is cool. If oven is still hot from convection or combination cooking, choose glass or oven-safe plastic containers. Refer to Cookware and Utensil Guide on page 5.
5. Cooktimes and food quantities given should be used as a guide. In microwaving, the greater the quantity of food the longer time it will take to cook.

FOOD		Cover	Power Level and Time	Comments
Appetizers	Party mix (2½-quarts)	No	High (10) 6 to 7 minutes.	Stir every 2 minutes.
	Meat balls, small meat or hot dog chunks (24)	Wax paper or plastic wrap	High (10) 5 to 6 minutes.	Spread in single layer in 2-quart oblong glass baking dish.
	Stuffed vegetables (12)	No	High (10) 3 to 4 minutes.	Space evenly on trivet or on plate lined with paper towels.
	Toasted nuts or seeds (½ to 1 cup)	No	High (10) 8 to 10 minutes.	Combine nuts with small amount of butter, stirring every 2 minutes.
Cakes, Cookies, Breads	Oblong, square or round	No	High (10) 2 minutes. Medium High (7) 3 to 5 minutes.	Rotate cake ½ turn; reduce power to Medium High (7) to complete cooking.
	Fluted tube cake	No	High (10) 12 to 14 minutes.	Rotate dish ½ turn after 6 minutes. Let stand 5 to 10 minutes before inverting.
	Cheesecake (9-in. pie plate)	No	Medium High (7) 12 to 14 minutes.	Microwave cheesecake mixture in 2-quart casserole until thick and smooth. Stir every 2 minutes with wire whisk. Pour into crumb crust. Refrigerate until firm.
	Bar Cookies (8-in. square dish)	No	High (10) 5 to 7 minutes.	Rotate ½ turn after 3 minutes.
	Muffins (6)	No	Medium High (7) 2 to 4 minutes.	Check at minimum time.
Eggs, Cheese, Dairy	Scrambled eggs	No	High (10) Allow 1 minute per egg.	Stir 2 or 3 times during microwaving.
	Quiche	No	Medium High (7) 16 to 21 minutes.	Pour filling into prebaked shell.
	Noodle or rice casseroles (2-quarts)	Lid or plastic wrap	High (10) 8 to 15 minutes.	Add ingredients to precooked pasta. Stir after ½ of cooking time. Add crumb topping just before serving.
	Thickened sauces and gravies (1 cup)	No	Medium (5) 3 to 5 minutes.	Microwave fat, flour and salt 1 to 2 minutes; stir to blend. Add liquid. Stir every minute.
	Scald milk (½ cup)	No	Medium High (7) 5 to 7 minutes.	
	Melt butter (½ cup)	No	High (10) ½ to 1 minute.	
	Soften cream cheese (8-oz.)	No	Low (3) ½ to 1 minute.	Remove foil wrapper before softening and place on microwave-safe plate.
Fish & Shellfish	Fillets or steaks (1-lb.)	Wax paper	High (10) 5 to 7 minutes.	Very delicate fish should be placed on trivet.
	Whole fish	Plastic wrap	High (10) 5 to 7 minutes per lb.	Shield head and tail with aluminum foil.
	Casserole, pre-cooked (2 to 3-quart)	Plastic wrap	High (10) 12 to 18 minutes.	
	Scallops, shrimp, peeled (1-lb.)	Plastic wrap	High (10) 5 to 7 minutes.	Brush with garlic butter before cooking.
Fruits	Baked apples or pears	Lid or plastic wrap	High (10) 2 to 4 minutes per piece.	Pierce fruit or peel to prevent bursting.

FOOD		Cover	Power Level and Time	Comments
Meat	Ground meat (1-lb.)	Lid or wax paper	High (10) 5 to 7 minutes.	Break up and stir every 2 minutes.
	Bacon (2 to 8 strips)	Paper towels	High (10) 1 minute per slice.	Put on trivet or on paper-towel-lined plate.
	Sausage	Wax paper	High (10) Patties: 1 minute per patty. Links: ½ to ¾ minutes per link.	Put on paper towel lined plate or glass dish. Turn over after half of cooking time.
	Franks or hot dogs (1-lb.)	Lid or wax paper	High (10) 7 to 9 minutes.	Add ¾ cup water. Rearrange after half of cooking time.
	Sandwiches	Wrap in paper towel	High (10) 1 to 2 minutes per sandwich.	
	Meat casseroles with pre-cooked meat and ingredients	Lid or plastic wrap	High (10) 13 to 19 minutes.	Stir once or twice.
	Meat casseroles with raw meat and vegetables	Lid or wax paper	Ground meat: High (10) 28 to 32 minutes. Less tender chunks: Medium (5) 70 to 80 minutes.	Rearrange or stir after half time.
	Meat patties (4 per 1-lb.)	Wax paper	High (10) 5 to 7 minutes.	Place on trivet or on paper towel-lined plate. Rearrange patties after 3 minutes.
	Meat loaf, beef or ham (1½-lbs. meat)	Plastic wrap	9-in. pie plate: High (10) 15 to 20 minutes. 9x5x3-in. loaf dish: Medium High (7) 25 to 30 minutes.	
	Braised (water cooked): short ribs, brisket, spare ribs (2 to 3-lbs.)	Lid or plastic wrap	Medium (5) 80 to 90 minutes.	Cover meat with water. Rearrange after half of cooking time. For ribs, drain 10 minutes before finishing; add barbecue sauce and finish.
	Chops with sauce (4 1-inch chops)	Wax paper	Medium High (7) 32 to 36 minutes.	Arrange in casserole. Turn over after half of cooking time.
Pasta	Long pieces (spaghetti, etc., ½-lb.)	Plastic wrap	High (10) 12 to 15 minutes.	In 2-quart oblong glass dish, add 6 cups hot tap water, 1 tablespoon oil, 1 teaspoon salt. Rearrange after half of cooking time.
	Cereal or instant rice	Lid or plastic wrap	High (10) 2 to 3 minutes per serving.	Add hot tap water as given on package. Stir after half of cooking time.
Pies	Crumb crust (9-in.)	No	Medium (5) 2 to 3 minutes.	Rotate dish ½ turn after 1 minute.
Poultry	Chicken, 6 to 8 pieces	Wax paper or plastic wrap	High (10) 15 to 18 minutes.	Turn over or rotate after half of cooking time.
	Chicken, whole or Cornish hens	Cooking Bag	Medium High (7) 10 to 12 minutes per lb.	Place on trivet. Turn over after half of cooking time. Shield tips of wings and legs with foil.
	Turkey legs or quarters	Cooking Bag	Medium (5) 12 to 14 minutes per lb.	Turn over after half of cooking time.
	Turkey breast	Cooking Bag	Medium (5) 10 to 12 minutes per lb.	Place on trivet, breast side down. Turn over after half of cooking time.
Roasts	Pot roast (3 to 4-lbs.)	Cooking Bag	Low (3) 20 to 23 minutes per lb.	Turn over after half of cooking time.
	Tender beef roast (rib-eye, bone-in rib, rolled rib)	Cooking Bag	Medium (5) Rare: 8 to 11 minutes per lb. Medium: 11 to 14 minutes per lb. Well done: 14 to 17 minutes per lb.	Turn over after half of cooking time.
	Pork roast	Cooking Bag	Medium (5) 14 to 17 minutes per lb.	Turn over after half of cooking time.
	Ham roast, pre-cooked	Plastic wrap or wax paper	Medium (5) 13 to 15 minutes per lb.	Turn over after half of cooking time.

Defrosting Chart *Power Level: Defrost (3)*

1. Most foods defrost well using Defrost (3). For more even defrosting of larger foods such as beef, lamb and veal roasts use Warm (1).
2. Most foods should be turned over or rearranged after half of defrosting time.

3. When defrosting steaks or chops, separate and remove defrosted pieces after half of defrost time. Allow these portions to stand on counter to complete defrosting and return frozen pieces to oven to complete defrosting.

FOOD		First Half Time, Min.	Second Half Time, Min.	Comments
Breads, Cakes	Bread or buns (1-lb. pkg.)	2	1 to 2	Turn over after first half of time.
	Heat & serve rolls (7-oz. pkg.)	1	1 to 2	Rotate ½ turn after first half of time.
	Coffee cake (11 to 13-oz.)	2	3 to 4	Rotate ½ turn after first half of time.
	Coffee ring (10-oz. pkg.)	2	1 to 2	Rotate ½ turn after first half of time.
	Sweet rolls (12-oz. pkg.)	1½	1 to 2	Rotate ½ turn after first half of time.
	Doughnuts (1 to 3)	½ to 1	none	No turn needed.
	Doughnuts, glazed (box of 12)	1	1 to 2	Rotate ½ turn after first half of time.
	French toast (2 slices)	1½	1½	Rotate ½ turn after first half of time.
	Cake, frosted 2 to 3 layer (17-oz.)	3	none	No turn needed. Let stand 5 to 10 minutes before serving.
	Cake, filled or topped 1 layer (12½ to 16-oz.)	1	1 to 2	Rotate ½ turn after first half of time. Let stand 5 to 10 minutes before serving.
	Pound cake (11¼-oz.)	2 to 4	none	No turn needed. Let stand 5 to 10 minutes before serving.
	Cheesecake, plain or fruit top (17 to 19-oz.)	2	2	Rotate ¼ turn after first half of time. Microwave 1 to 2 minutes more, if needed.
	Crunch cakes & cupcakes (1 to 2)	½ to 1	none	No turn needed.
	Fruit or nut pie (8-in.)	4	4 to 6	Rotate ½ turn after first half of time.
	Cream or custard pie (14-oz.)	1	1 to 2	Rotate ¼ turn after first half of time.
Fish & Seafood	Fillets (1-lb.)	4 to 5	5 to 7	Place unopened package in oven. (If fish is frozen in water, place in cooking dish.) Rotate ¼ turn after first half of time. After second half of time, hold under cold water to separate.
	Steaks (6-oz.)	2	1	Place wrapped steaks in oven. Rotate ¼ turn after first half of time.
	Whole fish (8 to 10-oz.)	2	3 to 4	Place fish in cooking dish. Turn over after first half of time. After second half of time, rinse cavity with cold water to complete defrosting.
	Shellfish, small pieces (1-lb.)	3 to 4	3 to 4	Spread shellfish in single layer in baking dish. Rearrange pieces after first half of time.
	Shellfish, blocks Crab meat (6-oz. pkg.)	2	2 to 3	Place block in casserole. Turn over and break up with fork after first half of time.
	Oysters (12-oz. can)	5 to 7	5 to 7	Place block in casserole. Turn over and break up with fork after first half of time.
	Scallops (1-lb. pkg.)	5 to 7	5 to 7	Place block in casserole. Turn over and break up with fork after first half of time.
	Shellfish, large Crab legs — 1 to 2 (8 to 10-oz.)	2 to 3	2 to 3	Arrange in cooking dish with light underside up. Turn over after first half of time.
	Lobster tails — 1 to 2 (6 to 9-oz.)	3 to 4	3 to 4	Arrange in cooking dish with light underside up. Turn over after first half of time.
	Whole lobster or crab (1½-lb.)	8 to 9	8 to 9	Place in cooking dish with light underside up. Turn over after first half of time.

FOOD		First Half Time, Min.	Second Half Time, Min.	Comments
Fruit	Fresh (10 to 16-oz.) (In microwave-safe container)	2 ½	2 ½	Place package in oven. After first half of time, break up with fork. Let stand on counter to complete defrosting.
	Plastic pouch — 1 to 2 (10-oz. pkg.)	2 ½	2 ½ to 5 ½	Place package in oven. After first half of time, flex package.
Meat	Bacon (1-lb.)	2 to 3 per lb.	2 to 3 per lb.	Place unopened package in oven. Turn over after first half of time. Microwave just until strips can be separated.
	Franks (1-lb.) (½-lb.)	1 to 2 1 ½ to 2 ½	1 to 2 none	Place unopened package in oven. Turn over after first half of time. Microwave just until franks can be separated.
	Ground beef or pork (1-lb.)	5	4	Scrape off meat that softens during defrosting. Set aside. Break up remaining block and continue defrosting.
	(1 ½ to 2-lbs.)	7	7	Scrape off meat that softens during defrosting. Set aside. Break up remaining block and continue defrosting.
	(5-lbs.)	13	13	Scrape off meat that softens during defrosting. Set aside. Break up remaining block and continue defrosting.
	Roast: beef, lamb or veal (3 to 5-lbs.)	Use Warm (1) for roasts 7 per lb.	7 per lb.	Place unwrapped roast in glass casserole. Turn over after first half of time. Let stand 30 minutes.
	Roast, pork (3 to 5-lbs.)	4 to 5 per lb.	4 to 5 per lb.	Place unwrapped roast in glass casserole. Turn over after first half of time. Let stand 30 minutes.
	Spareribs, pork (1 ½-lbs.)	2 to 4 per lb.	2 to 4 per lb.	Place wrapped package in oven. Turn over after first half of time. After second half of time, unwrap and separate pieces. Let stand to complete defrosting.
	Steaks, chops or cutlets: beef, lamb, pork & veal	3 to 5 per lb.	3 to 5 per lb.	Place wrapped package in oven. Turn over after first half of time. After second half of time, unwrap and separate pieces. Let stand to complete defrosting.
	Sausage, bulk (1-lb. roll)	2 to 3	2 to 3	Scrape off softened meat after second half of time. Set aside. Break up remaining block, microwave 2 to 3 minutes more, if needed.
	Sausage, link (½ to 1-lb.)	1 ½	1 to 2	Turn over after first half of time.
	Sausage, patties (12-oz. pkg.)	2	2 to 3	Turn over and separate after first half of time.
Poultry	Chicken, cut up (2 ½ to 3 ½-lbs.)	7 to 8	7 to 8	Place wrapped chicken in oven. After first half of time, unwrap and turn over. After second half of time, separate pieces and place in cooking dish. Microwave 2 to 4 minutes more, if necessary.
	Chicken, whole (2 ½ to 3 ½-lbs.)	10 to 12	10 to 12	Place wrapped chicken in oven. After first half of time unwrap and turn over. Shield warm areas with foil.
	Cornish hen	5 to 6 per lb.	5 to 6 per lb.	Place wrapped package in oven. Turn over after first half of time. After second half of time, unwrap and shield warm areas and ends of legs with foil. Microwave 3 to 4 minutes more, if necessary.
	Duckling	4 to 6 per lb.	4 to 6 per lb.	Place wrapped duckling in oven. After first half of time, unwrap, turn over and place in cooking dish. Shield warm areas and ends of legs with foil.
	Turkey breast	3 to 5 per lb.	3 to 5 per lb.	Place unwrapped turkey, breast side down, in cooking dish. After first half of time, turn turkey breast side up and shield with foil.

Heating or Reheating Chart

1. Directions below are for reheating already-cooked foods at refrigerator or room temperature. Use microwave oven-safe containers.
2. Cover most foods for fastest heating. Exceptions are rare or medium rare meats, some sandwiches, griddle foods like pancakes and baked foods.
3. Bubbling around edges of dish is normal, since center is last to heat. Stir foods before serving whenever possible.
4. Stir, rearrange, or rotate large amounts of food after half the suggested heating time.
5. Be sure foods are heated through before serving. Steaming or bubbling around edges does not necessarily mean food is heated throughout. As a general rule, hot foods produce an area warm to the touch in center of underside of dish.
6. When covering with plastic wrap, turn back one corner to vent.

Item		Amount	Power Level	Approx. Time, Minutes
Appetizers	Saucy such as: meatballs, riblets, cocktail franks, etc.	1 to 2 servings	High (10)	2 to 3
	½ cup / serving	3 to 4 servings	High (10)	5 to 6
	Dips: cream or process cheese	½ cup	Medium (5)	2½ to 3
		1 cup	Medium (5)	3 to 4
	Pastry bites: small pizzas, egg rolls etc.	2 to 4 servings	High (10)	2 to 3
	Tip: Cover saucy appetizers with wax paper. Cover dips with plastic wrap. Do not cover pastry bites.			
Plate of Leftovers	Meat plus 2 vegetables	1 to 2 plates	High (10)	3 to 4
	Tip: Cover plate of food with wax paper or plastic wrap.			
Meats & Main Dishes	Saucy Main Dishes: chop suey, spaghetti, creamed chicken, chili, stew, macaroni and cheese, etc.	1 to 2 servings	High (10)	3 to 6
		3 to 4 servings	High (10)	9 to 12
	¾-1 cup / serving	1 16-oz. can	High (10)	5 to 7
	Thinly sliced roasted meat: Rare, minimum time	1 to 2 servings	Medium High (7)	1 to 3
	Medium Rare, maximum time	3 to 4 servings	Medium High (7)	2 to 4
	3 to 4-oz. / serving			
	Well done beef, pork, ham, poultry, etc.	1 to 2 servings	Medium High (7)	1 to 3
	3 to 4-oz. / serving	3 to 4 servings	Medium High (7)	3 to 5
	Steaks, chops, ribs, other meat pieces:			
	Rare beef steak	1 to 2 servings	Medium High (7)	2 to 4
		3 to 4 servings	Medium High (7)	5 to 7
	Well done beef, chops, ribs, etc.	1 to 2 servings	Medium High (7)	2 to 3
		4 servings	Medium High (7)	6 to 7
	Hamburgers or meat loaf	1 to 2 servings	High (10)	1 to 2
	4-oz. / serving	3 to 4 servings	High (10)	2 to 4
	Chicken pieces	1 to 2 pieces	High (10)	1 to 2
		3 to 4 pieces	High (10)	2 to 3
	Hot dogs and sausages	1 to 2	High (10)	½ to 1½
		3 to 4	High (10)	1½ to 2½
	Rice and pasta Plain or buttered	1 to 2 servings	High (10)	1 to 3
	½ to 1 cup / serving	3 to 4 servings	High (10)	3 to 5
	Topped or mixed with sauce	1 to 2 servings	High (10)	4 to 6
	½ to 1 cup / serving	3 to 4 servings	High (10)	8 to 10
	Tip: Cover saucy main dishes with plastic wrap. Cover other main dishes and meats with wax paper. Do not cover rare or medium rare meats.			

Item		Amount	Power Level	Approx. Time, Minutes
Sandwiches	Moist filling			
	sloppy joe, barbecue, ham salad, etc. in bun	1 to 2 servings	Medium High (7)	1 to 2
	⅓ cup / serving	3 to 4 servings	Medium High (7)	2 to 4
	Thick meat-cheese filling with firm bread	1 to 2 servings	Medium High (7)	1 to 3
		3 to 4 servings	Medium High (7)	3 to 5
	Soup			
	Water based 1 cup / serving	1 to 2 servings	High (10)	1 to 3
		3 to 4 servings	High (10)	3 to 6
		1 10-oz. can reconstituted	High (10)	3 to 5
	Milk based 1 cup / serving	1 to 2 servings	Medium High (7)	2 to 4
		3 to 4 servings	Medium High (7)	6 to 10
		1 10-oz. can reconstituted	Medium High (7)	6 to 8
	Tip: Use paper towel or napkin to cover sandwiches. Cover soups with wax paper or plastic wrap.			
Vegetables	Small pieces			
	peas, bean, corn, etc.	1 to 2 servings	High (10)	1 to 3
	½ cup / serving	3 to 4 servings	High (10)	2 to 3
		1 16-oz. can	High (10)	2 to 4
	Large pieces or whole	1 to 2 servings	High (10)	2 to 3
	asparagus spears, corn on the cob, etc.	3 to 4 servings	High (10)	3 to 4
		1 16-oz. can	High (10)	4
	Mashed potatoes, squash, pumpkin, etc.	1 to 2 servings	High (10)	1 to 3
	½ cup / serving	3 to 4 servings	High (10)	4 to 7
	Tip: Cover vegetables for most even heating.			
Sauces	Dessert: chocolate or butterscotch	½ cup	High (10)	1 to 2
		1 cup	High (10)	2 to 3
	Meat or main dish, chunky type	½ cup	High (10)	1 to 2
	giblet gravy, spaghetti sauce, etc.	1 cup	High (10)	2 to 3
		1 16-oz. can	High (10)	5 to 6
	Creamy type	½ cup	High (10)	1 to 1½
		1 cup	High (10)	2 to 2½
	Tip: Cover food to prevent spatter.			
Bakery Foods	Cake, coffee cake, doughnuts, sweet rolls, nut or fruit bread	1 piece	Low (3)	½ to 1
		2 pieces	Low (3)	1 to 1½
		9-in. cake or 12 rolls or doughnuts	Low (3)	2 to 4
	Dinner rolls, muffins	1	Medium (5)	¼ to ½
		2 to 4	Medium (5)	½ to 1
		6 to 8	Medium (5)	1 to 2
	Pie fruit, nut or custard	1 slice	High (10)	½ to 1
	⅛ of 9-in. pie = 1 slice	2 slices	High (10)	1 to 1½
	(use minimum time for custard)	9-in. pie	Medium High (7)	5 to 7
Griddle Foods	Pancakes, French toast or waffles (3″ x 4″)			
	Plain, no topping	2 or 3 pieces	High (10)	½ to 1
	With syrup & butter	2 or 3 pieces	High (10)	1 to 2
	With 2 sausage patties (cooked)	2 or 3 pieces	High (10)	1 to 2
Beverages	Coffee, tea, cider, other water based	1 to 2 cups	High (10)	1 to 3
		3 to 4 cups	High (10)	6 to 7
	Cocoa, other milk based	1 to 2 cups	Medium High (7)	3 to 5
		3 to 4 cups	Medium High (7)	6 to 9

Convection Baking Chart

1. Always use metal accessory rack when convection baking. (See Use & Care Book.)
2. Aluminum pans conduct heat quickly. For most convection baking, light shiny finishes give best results because they prevent overbrowning in the time it takes for heat to cook the center areas. Dull (satin-finish) bottom surfaces of pans are recommended for cake pans and pie plates to be sure those areas brown completely.
3. Dark or non-shiny finishes, also glass and pyroceram, absorb heat which may result in dry, crisp crusts.
4. Preheating the oven is recommended when baking foods by convection.
5. Open the oven door to check food as little as possible to prevent uneven heating and to save energy.

FOOD		Oven Temp.	Time, Min.	Comments
Breads	Biscuits	400°	12 to 15	Canned refrigerated biscuits take 2 to 4 minutes less time.
	Corn Bread	400°	15 to 20	
	Muffins	375°	15 to 19	Remove from pans immediately and cool slightly on wire rack.
	Popovers	350°	30 to 40	Prick each popover with a fork after removing from oven to allow steam to escape.
	Nut Bread or Fruit Bread	350°	40 to 60	Interiors will be moist and tender.
	Yeast Bread	375°	18 to 25	
	Plain or Sweet Rolls	350°	13 to 16	Lightly grease baking sheet.
Cakes	Angel Food	325°	30 to 40	Invert and cool in pan.
	Cheesecake	325°	60 to 65	After cooking, turn oven off and let cheesecake stand in oven 30 minutes with door ajar.
	Coffee Cake	350°	25 to 30	
	Cup Cakes	325°	15 to 20	
	Fruit Cake (loaf)	275°	80 to 90	Interior will be moist and tender.
	Gingerbread	350°	35 to 40	
	Jelly Roll	350°	12 to 14	
	Butter Cakes (2 layers)	325°	30 to 40	
	Cake Mixes (2 layers)	325°	30 to 40	
	Fluted Tube Cake	325°	40 to 50	Grease and flour pan.
	Pound Cake	325°	60 to 70	Cool in pan 10 minutes before inverting on wire rack.
Cookies	Bar	350°	35 to 45	Use same time for bar cookies from a mix.
	Drop or Sliced	350°	13 to 15	Use same time for sliced cookies from a mix.

Convection Baking Chart *continued*

FOOD		Oven Temp.	Time, Min.	Comments
Fruits, Other Desserts	Baked Apples or Pears	350°	30 to 40	Bake in utensil with shallow sides.
	Bread Pudding	300°	35 to 40	Pudding is done when knife inserted near center comes out clean.
	Cream Puffs	400°	25 to 30	Puncture puffs twice with toothpick to release steam after 15 minutes of baking time.
	Custard (individual)	300°	35 to 40	Set cups in baking dish. Pour boiling water around cups to a depth of 1 inch.
	Fruit Compote	325°	30 to 35	
	Meringue Shells	275°	30 to 35	When done, turn oven off and let shells stand in oven 1 hour to dry.
Pies, Pastries	Frozen	375°	40 to 45	Follow procedure on package.
	Meringue-topped	325°	13 to 16	
	Two-crust	375°	50 to 55	
	Quiche	350°	30 to 40	Let stand 10 minutes before cutting.
	Pastry Shell	400°	10 to 16	Prick pastry with fork to prevent shrinkage.
Casseroles	Meat, chicken, seafood combinations	325°	20 to 40	Cook times vary with casserole size and ingredients.
	Pasta	350°	25 to 45	Cook times vary with casserole size and ingredients.
	Potatoes, scalloped	350°	55 to 60	Let stand 5 minutes before serving.
	Vegetable	350°	25 to 35	Cook times vary with casserole size and ingredients.
Convenience Foods	Frozen Bread Dough	325°	30 to 35	
	Frozen Dinners	350°	20 to 25	Follow package directions.
	Frozen Entrees	350°	50 to 60	Follow package directions.
	Frozen Pizza Rolls, Egg Rolls	400°	8 to 10	Follow package directions.
	Pizza	375°	20 to 22	
	Slice and Bake Cookies	325°	13 to 15	Let stand a few minutes on baking sheet before removing to cool.
Main Dishes	Meat Loaf	350°	55 to 60	
	Oven-baked Stew	325°	80 to 90	Brown meat before combining with liquid and vegetables.
	Swiss Steak	325°	60 to 70	
	Stuffed Peppers	350°	40 to 45	Use green, red or yellow peppers.
Vegetables	Acorn Squash	350°	50 to 60	Turn squash halves cut side up after 30 minutes of cook time.
	Baked Potatoes	400°	45 to 50	Prick skins with a fork before baking.
	Twice-Baked Potatoes	400°	20 to 25	

Meat Roasting Chart for Convection Cooking

MEATS		Minutes / Lb.	Oven Temp.	Internal Temp
Beef	Rib (3 to 5-lbs.)			
	Rare	25 to 30	325°	140°
	Medium	30 to 35	325°	160°
	Well	35 to 40	325°	170°
	Boneless Rib, Top Sirloin			
	Rare	25 to 30	325°	140°
	Medium	30 to 35	325°	160°
	Well	35 to 40	325°	170°
	Beef Tenderloin			
	Rare	15 to 19	325°	140°
	Medium	19 to 23	325°	160°
	Pot Roast (2 ½ to 3-lbs.)			
	Chuck, Rump	40 to 45	300°	170°
Ham	Canned (3-lb. fully cooked)	18 to 21	325°	140°
	Butt (5-lb. fully cooked)	18 to 21	325°	140°
	Shank (5-lb. fully cooked)	18 to 21	325°	140°
Lamb	Bone-in (3 to 5-lbs.)			
	Medium	25 to 30	325°	160°
	Well	30 to 35	325°	170°
	Boneless (3 to 5-lbs.)			
	Medium	25 to 30	325°	160°
	Well	30 to 35	325°	170°
Pork	Bone-in (3 to 5-lbs.)	29 to 33	325°	170°
	Boneless (3 to 5-lbs.)	29 to 33	325°	170°
	Pork Chops (½ to 1-inch thick)			
	2 chops	35 to 40 total	325°	170°
	4 chops	40 to 45 total	325°	170°
	6 chops	45 to 50 total	325°	170°
Poultry	Whole Chicken	50 to 60 total	350°	180° to 185°
	(2 ½ to 3 ½ lbs.)			
	Chicken Pieces	35 to 45 total	350°	180° to 185°
	(2 ½ to 3 ½ lbs.)			
	Cornish Hens			
	Unstuffed (1 to 1 ½ lbs.)	55 to 50 total	350°	180° to 185°
	Stuffed (1 to 1 ½ lbs.)	60 to 65 total	350°	180° to 185°
	Duckling (4 to 5 lbs.)	24 to 26 total	350°	180° to 185°
	Turkey Breast	23 to 30 total	325°	170°
	(4 to 6 lbs.)			
Seafood	Fish, whole	30 to 40 total	400°	
	(3 to 5 lbs)			
	Lobster Tails	20 to 25 total	350°	
	(6 to 8-oz. each)			

Meat Roasting Chart for Combination Cooking

MEATS		Combination Temperature	Minutes / Lb.	Temperature or Probe Setting
Beef	Rib (3 to 5-lbs.)			
	Rare	325°	10 to 14	140°
	Medium	325°	14 to 18	160°
	Well	325°	18 to 22	170°
	Boneless Rib, Top Sirloin			
	Rare	325°	10 to 14	140°
	Medium	325°	14 to 18	160°
	Well	325°	18 to 22	170°
	Beef Tenderloin			
	Rare	325°	10 to 14	140°
	Medium	325°	14 to 18	160°
	Pot Roast (2 ½ to 3-lbs.)			
	Chuck, Rump	275°	1 ¾ to 2 hours total	170°
	Turn meat over after half of cooking time.			
Ham	Canned (3-lb. fully cooked)	325°	14 to 17	140°
	Butt (5-lb. fully cooked)	325°	14 to 17	140°
	Shank (5-lb. fully cooked)	325°	14 to 17	140°
Lamb	Bone-in (3 to 5-lbs.)			
	Medium	325°	14 to 19	140°
	Well	325°	19 to 24	160°
	Boneless (3 to 5-lbs.)			
	Medium	325°	14 to 19	140°
	Well	325°	19 to 24	160°
Pork	Bone-in (3 to 5-lbs.)	325°	14 to 18	170°
	Boneless (3 to 5-lbs.)	325°	14 to 18	170°
	Pork Chops (½ to 1-inch thick)			
	2 chops	350°	29 to 34 total	
	4 chops	350°	35 to 40 total	
	6 chops	350°	41 to 46 total	
Poultry	Whole Chicken (2 ½ to 3 ½ lbs.)	375°	45 to 50 total	180° to 185°
	Chicken Pieces (2 ½ to 3 ½ lbs.)	375°	35 to 40 total	180° to 185°
	Cornish Hens			
	Unstuffed	375°	50 to 55 total	180° to 185°
	Stuffed	375°	55 to 60 total	180° to 185°
	Duckling	375°	60 to 70 total	180° to 185°
	Turkey Breast (4 to 6 lbs.)	325°	16 to 20	170°
Seafood	Fish 1-lb. fillets	350°	7 to 10 total	
	Lobster Tails (6 to 8-oz. each)	350°	13 to 18 total	
	Shrimp (1 to 2-lbs.)	350°	10 to 13 total	
	Scallops (1 to 2-lbs.)	350°	10 to 13 total	

Index

CREDITS:
Wendy Shafer Shirrell, Editor
Manager, Consumer Information
Testing Laboratory
GE Appliances

Thanks To Home Economists:
Brigid Lally Bowles
Cynthia Fanning Forester

Design, Production, Photography
and Food Styling:
OTT Communications, Inc.
Louisville, Kentucky